Fifty Tales for a Grey Windy Weekend in Ardnamurchan
and Ten for the Wet Monday

Fifty Tales for a
Grey Windy Weekend
in Ardnamurchan
and Ten for the
Wet Monday

Tom Carbery

Kennedy & Boyd

Kennedy & Boyd
an imprint of
Zeticula Ltd
The Roan,
Kilkerran,
KA19 8LS
Scotland.

http://www.kennedyandboyd.co.uk
admin@kennedyandboyd.co.uk

First published in 2012
Copyright © Thomas F. Carbery 2012
Cover photograph © ???

ISBN 978-1-84921-117-8

Acknowledgements

The acknowledgements which are appropriate to this, my second book of assorted tales, are very similar to those which appeared in the first book, which was published in 2010.

I continue to be indebted to Mr Peter Donnelly and my former colleague, Mr John C McIntyre, for their encouragement to embark on and to continue with this venture.

The word processing was originally undertaken by Mrs Susan McCourt and our eldest grand-child, Jennifer Carbery. The bulk of this work was taken over by Mrs Alyson Taylor. I gratefully thank all three for their patience and forbearance.

Mr McIntyre undertook almost all the editorial work and has been of tremendous assistance, without his efforts, the book would never have been published. He joins me in hoping that this volume produces the same amount of smiles, chuckles, laughs and tears as did the first book.

T. F. Carbery
Glasgow,
September, 2012

Contents

Fifty Tales for a Grey Windy Weekend in Ardnamurchan
and Ten for the Wet Monday

Reserves of Labour

My last year in the Ministry of Labour was my worst. It would be wrong, however, to infer that it was that bad year, and it had been a very heavy, demanding rather unpleasant year, which drove me out of what had been happy, enjoyable and above all satisfying employment. Truth to tell, I had been teaching two or three evenings each week through the academic year at the Scottish College of Commerce and had found it most rewarding: in other words I was not averse to a switch to teaching.

The "bad" year ran from the summer of 1960 to the same season in 1961. In 1954 I had been fortunate enough to be promoted from Clerical Officer to the rank of Junior Executive Officer and had spent six years as an Insurance Officer under the provisions of the National Insurance Act of 1946. This meant that I was empowered to resolve doubtful claims for Unemployment Benefit and appear for the Department before Insurance Appeal Tribunals and, beyond that, appear at hearings before the National Insurance Commissioner.

There had been three small breaks in this experience. Firstly, I had three weeks in Fraserburgh endeavouring to interview "share fishermen" about the working and fairness of the specific Regulations which applied to them. This had been a total disaster in that I did not understand them and they, in turn, did not understand me and this despite my attempting to sound like a BBC announcer reading the Shipping Forecast.

Later I had four weeks in our Scottish Headquarters in Edinburgh while the last of these secondments was a three week spell as the Acting Manager of Dumbarton Employment Exchange, the unfortunate Manager having taken a Boys' Brigade company to camp in Jersey where he had died.

Early in 1960 I had been put up for promotion but had been unsuccessful. In the wake of this disappointment two explanations were forthcoming, one well-nigh immediately and the other in due course. The immediate disclosure was that I had been deemed to have insufficient experience of supervision of staff – the three weeks' managerial experience in Dumbarton and a one-third share of a Clerical Assistant being regarded as inadequate. The other explanation of my non-promotion was longer in forthcoming and when it did emerge was more distressing and disconcerting.

During my six years as an Insurance Officer we had two managers, Alex Lambie having been succeeded by Miss Dickson. We knew that this was the lady's first appointment following her recent promotion. It soon transpired she was woefully lacking in confidence. What we had not known at the time was how considerable this was. In the wake of my non-promotion, she had asked Mr Lambie to leave, for her to see and use, his assessment of the staff of the office. As a result when after six months or so in post she had been due to submit her assessment of our performance she slavishly copied the Lambie evaluation and sent it off in the happy confidence that no-one would question what purported to be her assessment. A year later she did it again.

Now Alex Lambie had been of an old school which subscribed to the view that nobody, however good at the job, was worthy of further promotion until he or she had done five years in his/her existing grade.

Here it should be explained that those reporting on staff had four options, i.e.

Not yet qualified for promotion	(NQ)
Qualified for promotion	(Q3)
Well qualified for promotion	(Q2)
Exceptionally well qualified	(Q1)

Subscribing as he did to the old tradition, Lambie had shown me as "Not yet qualified" and so too Miss Dickson, not once but twice. Then, in the following year, the year of the promotion panel, she had put me in as Q1 – exceptionally well qualified. The result of that action was that all hell was let loose and a senior officer at Scottish HQ called her through to Edinburgh to explain this remarkable transformation, whereupon, in her embarrassment and confusion and through her tears, she poured out the story of her ploy involving Alex Lambie.

It was said later, as the story slowly emerged, that the senior staffing officer wiped the floor with her, and said that he would do what he could to sort it out, but that there could be no promotion for the young man in that calendar year.

These then were the circumstances which constituted the background to my being transferred from my comfy, cosy, competent existence in what was called the Group Insurance Office in the middle of Glasgow to an Employment Exchange in the north-west sector of the conurbation. And what an Exchange it was. It was not the building or the clients or the broad sweep of the staff that caused eyebrows to quiver and strong men to shiver. The cause of such phenomena was the presence and personality of its manager, a certain – and she was always certain and never in doubt – Miss Ethel Dorman.

Miss Dorman was to the Ministry of Labour what Captain Bligh was to the Royal Navy. The Lords of the Admiralty saw Bligh as an exemplary seaman and officer, reliable and loyal. To them he was a first-class example of how to run a ship, a shade hard perhaps but invariably anxious to please those in high command. The same man was seen by those who had the misfortune to serve under him as two notches away from being a tyrant. A man who delighted, who revelled in having a reputation for being a hard man who ran his ship and crew to the very edges of cruelty.

As a young woman in the Civil Service and within the Ministry of Labour, Miss Dorman had won early promotion to Junior Executive status and thereafter served in a variety of Exchanges in the course of which she served in every post, in every section of an Exchange. As she herself was prone to remark, there was no task in an Exchange which could be entrusted to an executive which she had not undertaken. In short, she had done it all and although she did not add it, it was to be taken that she had done everything not just well, but wonderfully well. There was no questioning this account of her early to middle career though it was not easily reconciled with her rather late promotion to Grade 4 or Higher Executive Officer and that she had never been promoted beyond that grade.

When she had risen to HEO she had served first as Deputy Manager in a big Exchange in Glasgow and then being deemed ready "for her own ship", so to speak, had been manager in two Exchanges, one in Lanarkshire and the other, slightly bigger, in Renfrewshire before moving to her then current post. When I arrived she was due to retire some seven or eight years down the road. It was said that there were those who prayed fervently for that happy day.

On moving from my confident, competent comfort zone of the Group Insurance Office in the centre of town to the tenemental terrain of the north-west, I felt like a man from New York or Boston being sent in the late 19th century to Wyoming to deal with cattlemen fighting with farmers over water rights while having to cope with bands of marauding Indians and all the while being under the jurisdiction of a rather nasty and not exactly congenial sheriff. Then again, the travelling was not all that difficult but it was far from easy. I was to find that to be sure of being in the office for 9 a.m. I had to leave home no later than 7.20.

When I did arrive on my first day I was told to report to Miss Dorman in her office. She was almost gracious. She arranged for us to have tea and she invited me to sit. The only other occasion on which I was allowed to speak to her while seated was the day when I called to say goodbye.

At that first meeting she told me that the total staff was just over thirty, there were five Junior Executives or Grade 5 officers. She also said that a lady in the Insurance section was the senior of the five and therefore due to be the Deputy Manager but that she would be retiring shortly and had declined the honour. Inconsistently, the lady in question would act as manager when Miss Dorman herself was absent. Mr Archibald, the Finance Officer, was on the Grade 4 Waiting List and was liable to disappear any day now. So, she declared, I would work with her and be responsible for the first draft of the monthly reports and, on her behalf, I would visit employers to discuss employment and economic prospects. She observed *en passant* that it would all stand me in good stead.

As for my day-to-day work I was to be the supervisor in the Vacancy Section which to add to my delights was the first "integrated" such section in the Glasgow Area. Hitherto, men and women had been dealt with separately. To cope with this I would have a staffing allowance of 5.4 which included me as one of the five.

As things stood our total adult unemployment for our area was just over 1,800, our area running from St. George's Cross on the edge of the city centre to Drymen, well on the way to the Highlands.

As the interview progressed, Miss Dorman started to revel in her "obiter dicta". She told me that she had heard great things about me. Her friend, Miss Dickson, had been singing my praises, so much so that she, Miss Dorman, had been at a loss to comprehend why I had not been successful at the recent Promotions Panel. "There must be a flaw in you. It will be my job to find it and eradicate it and I promise you I shall do just that!" As she went on she declared that no-one in the whole of Scotland knew the working of the Exchanges better than she did. She knew where all the skeletons lay: it was invaluable information and with such knowledge one could make or break any officer. "Before you leave me I shall tell you how it can be done. But," she said, "that is for later. For the immediate future you must be at the receiving end of my policy and my methods." She concluded by observing that she was not as candid and forthcoming with all new members of her staff, I should regard myself as privileged.

I soon got to know my closest colleagues. Miss Sim was the most senior female Clerical Officer in the whole of Scotland. She lived nearby and had no interest in promotion and did not want any additional responsibility. She knew her job and could be a good and reliable worker. But she worked like a metronome, which meant she had one pace and rigidly adhered to it. The queues could be out the door and along the pavement but Miss Sim ignored them and proceeded to work and work accurately and well but at her own pace. When I foolishly exhorted her to step up her pace she would respond with a scowl, and thereupon lift her packet of cigarettes and her lighter and disappear into the Ladies' toilet with the result that the counter situation worsened rather than improved. My only further action worsened the situation yet again. The 0.4 on my staffing allowance was a nineteen-year-old girl called Deirdre. If I sent her into the Ladies to advise Miss Sim that she was needed, the outcome was that the veteran would persuade Deirdre to occupy the adjoining cubicle and reward her by rolling in the lighter and a cigarette, whereupon I was then two down on my complement.

Then there were the men, three of them. Two of them were in their middle to late fifties. They had been recruited as Temporary Clerks during the war when the Department had expanded very considerably. Later they had been established as Clerical Assistants and, later still, promoted to Clerical Officers. I was to find they were good, conscientious, hard-working officers.

The best of the four clerks, however, was a man a few years older than myself, called John Devine. Like me he had attended a good Senior Secondary. Like me, he had been in the Forces during the war and had served over five years. He too had sat the Civil Service Reconstruction Examination and, on learning of his success, had expressed a preference for the Ministry of Labour. It transpired he had been "up" for promotion and had been deemed to have been a near-miss candidate last time round. So it was that no other Clerical Officer being seen as a candidate for promotion, John was seen as my deputy.

Two weeks after I took over, Miss Dorman swept into our "section" and plunged into our filing cabinets. She started writing Error Sheets. Within minutes she was almost throwing them over her shoulder, meantime giving voice to little cries of delight. The sheets she left for me all called for immediate action. As she passed me she smiled and said: "Well, now, that little flurry will keep you out of mischief." She walked a little nearer the door and then came back to half-whisper: "Now you see what I mean about skeletons!"

Having sorted out the Error Sheets and rummaged in the files for other errors from yesteryears, I at last managed to get around to appraising the employment prospects of our customers. The more I examined the files the more I reckoned that the 1,800 could, fairly easily, be reduced to about 1,500. More, I took the view that we could get down to between 1,200 and 1,300, though this would involve us, ideally all of us, working more intensely than seemed to have been the norm.

Yet the situation was even more daunting in that I figured that it would be possible to drag our total unemployed below a thousand! To do that would involve a tremendous effort on the part of the staff. But how to motivate my colleagues? Persuasion, even eloquent persuasion, would not do it. So it was I had recourse to bribery.

I gathered them round me, advised them of my vision and hastened on to say that in the event of our getting down to three numerals I, out of my own resources, would pay for all of us to have dinner in the Berkeley Restaurant, just up from the Mitchell Library. The set dinner of three courses and coffee cost twelve shillings and sixpence a head, so allowing for the tip, success in this venture would cost me just over £4. To my surprise and delight they bought it!

Over the ensuing two months our register dropped and dropped and dropped. We had it down to just over 1,400 and further reduction seemed certain.

And then the Great Exercise blew up in our faces. It was a normal busy afternoon. Our "outside" phone rang. John Devine answered it. He indicated the call was for me. The caller was a friend of mine in Bridgeton Exchange on the other side of town.

"Tom," started my friend, "are you standing or sitting? If you are standing I think you had better get a chair."

Thereupon he advised me that Rose's Homes Ltd was closing its residence at 4 Craignestock Street. Worse: it was recommending to its residents that they should transfer to the company's other Glasgow establishment on the Garscube Road which was in our area. An influx, indeed, a substantial influx was imminent!

Perhaps it should be explained here that the establishment mentioned was one of what were known as "model lodging houses" of which there were seven in the Bridgeton area. Some were run by the local authority, some by Voluntary Bodies such as the Salvation Army and the rest by commercial undertakings such as Rose's Homes.

The day following that of the telephone call from Bridgeton, Glaswegians going about their business in the City Centre were liable to be confronted with scenes reminiscent of events in the First World War.

During that dreadful war and in particular during and in the wake of the really horrendous battles such as those on the Somme and at Ypres and Mons, British newspapers and the *Illustrated London News* provided photographs of blinded and other "walking wounded" being led in long single lines, each man with one hand on the shoulder of the man in front of him.

What Glasgow saw that day was very akin to such episodes: it was scenes of the residents of the Craignestock Street Model being escorted to their new hostel off the Garscube Road in what was known as The Big Mill though the noun was generally pronounced as "Mull".

Those who witnessed these events reckoned that over 600 men were involved but friends in the Bridgeton Exchange reckoned it was about 450. The bit that impacted on us was that when we opened our door the next day 260 fell in on us and at the same time destroyed all hope of our getting our total registered unemployed down to three numerals.

It took about a week or so for all the relevant documentation to come through from Bridgeton. When it did arrive each man's file was the size of a family Bible. I decided to go through them myself and in doing so put them in two piles, the first being of men who had done no work whatsoever over the preceding five years. There were nearly seventy in that group. The others had done some work even if it amounted to no more than once a year selling programmes at the Scottish Cup Final.

I sent for John and told him I would attend to the first group and asked him to take the others and share them out between himself and the three others. So it was I encountered Mr James Gunn.

I can see it yet. We had a small private room in which we could conduct all sensitive interviews. There I tried to put Mr Gunn at some ease and having done so observed that according to his file he had last worked in 1923. Was that correct? He did not know but said it was probably right. I asked if he could recall working? He said he couldn't.

I pointed out as reasonably as I could that I would give him from 1923 through the Twenties and through the Great Depression and all the Thirties. More, I would give him from the outbreak of the war in '39 and through to '41 as it took us until then to become fully geared for our war effort. Then again I would give him from the cessation of hostilities in '45 right up to that very day in 1960. But all that said, there was a mystery. From 1941 until 1945 he had been worth his wages plus 10% to any employer with a war contract. Even if he had spent every day hiding in the toilets he would have been worth his wages and the profit of the 10%.

"How did you avoid working then?" I asked.

He growled and glowered at me. "It wisnae easy!" he declared, "the polis kept moving us oan, so they did!"

As I travelled home that night I realised I was angry and angrier as I did not know what gave rise to that condition. Then it all fell into place.

Earlier that week I had heard a radio programme in which there had been a report of a speech in the Commons by a trade union-sponsored Labour M.P. He was a Scot who represented an English constituency. I knew him having met him at diverse week-end schools. The essence of his speech had been a spirited appeal to the Government to provide more resources to enable the unemployed to return to profitable employment. As he developed his argument the unemployed were all conscientious and eager to return to work. More, he contended that were this to be done it would add to our G.D.P and so increase the total prosperity while this increase in our national income flow would more than cover the cost of the extra expense of the overall exercise.

What he did not say was where the extra jobs were to be found. The next morning, sitting in the office, I found myself reflecting again and again on the void, the dichotomy, the gulf of Pacific

Ocean proportions between the economic situation portrayed by the Labour M.P and the reality of the situation as represented by our Mr Gunn.

Yes, there were able-bodied talented folk who were anxious and keen to return to gainful work and my colleagues and our counterparts were endeavouring to help them achieve their aspirations. But to suggest that all the unemployed were in this category was nonsense to the nth power.

Mr Gunn would never work again! Moreover, he had long ago exhausted any insurance benefit to which he was entitled. For years and years he had been financed by the National Assistance Board which had issued 'orders' for us to pay on their behalf. In some eighteen to twenty months he would reach retiral age whereupon the Board would make alternative arrangements to pay him and all connection with us would cease. As I saw it, Gunn had already retired.

So it was that foolishly, indeed rather stupidly, I wrote a letter – the sort of letter one should write but never send.

Miss Dorman was on holiday and the lady from the Insurance Section who was the Acting Manager had gone for three days to attend a cousin's funeral in Elgin. The next in command was the Finance Officer and he had phoned in to say he had a tummy upset. The result was that I took my hand-written letter to the Secretary and had her prepare four copies. One went to the local N.A.B., one to our Scottish H.Q., one for the files of our office and one copy for myself. Within 48 hours all hell broke loose.

It was argued I had gone well out of line. Who was I to question the existing well-tried arrangements? What I had done was equivalent to a young lieutenant writing to High Command questioning the validity of both our strategy and our tactics.

When Miss Dorman returned she solemnly wiped the floor with me, then descended to our section and threw a flood of further error sheets at me, snorted and left. And in one sense that is it! In one sense that was and is the story of the supposed reserves of labour, the story of the suggestion that poor James Gunn and other sad, woeful, woebegone souls were like the favourite at the local dog racing track, straining to get out and into dramatic action.

And yet there are tail-pieces to our tale. Firstly, it should be reported that for three weeks or so Miss Dorman ostracized me but in fairness it should be recorded that she mellowed. As the Presidential Election in the States approached, she increasingly found opportunities to lure me into discussion though such exchanges proved to be fraught, a situation caused by her rooting for Nixon while I favoured Kennedy. She explained that Nixon was the Vice President and so had experience for which there was no substitute. I told her I saw Tricky Dicky as opportunistic, a man whose career was fated to end in disaster.

One day, in the early autumn of 1960 an incident took place which illustrated the intolerance and, harsh though it is to say it, the ignorance of the lady.

I had been summoned to her room as she was concerned lest Brechin's, one of the biggest concerns in our area, was liable to pay off some workers or feel obliged to put some on part-time working. I, of course, was standing while she sat regally emanating unfailing confidence in her own views.

Suddenly she broke away from the main — until then the sole — topic of conversation to pronounce in a most aggrieved tone: "... and as for that Communist Kelly, he is driving me to distraction."

"Kelly? Kelly?" I ventured. "Do you mean the gentleman in the Insurance Section? For if you do, Miss Dorman, I can assure he is no Communist. He is not even in the ILP. Indeed, I do not believe he is a Labour Party member, though I would have taken it that he votes Labour."

"Don't you try to tell me who is and who is not a Communist!" she roared. "On that matter of the overtime he was positively obstructive. He refused to co-operate and agree to what I as a Manager deemed to be essential."

"Miss Dorman," I ventured, "he is the office representative of the Staff Association and all he was wanting was us, as the management team, to adhere to the terms of the Agreement on Overtime agreed by both the Association and the Department."

"But it was an emergency," she cried.

"And it was the section on emergencies to which he referred," I countered.

"This is too much," she ventured. "Now even my executives cannot see or refuse to see Communist activity when it is abundantly clear before their very eyes."

As the winter progressed it brought a flurry of pleasing occasions if not quite victories. It so happened that we had a local factory which over the years had experienced difficulty in keeping a suitable storeman. When they recruited a good one he would leave for more money elsewhere: when they got a bad one they had to sack him.

One day their Personnel Manager came on the phone to say it had happened again. He asked me to trawl and send some folk for interview. So I trawled. Having done so I phoned him and asked whether it had to be a man. He asked if I had a competent robot. I told him what I had for him was a very intelligent and capable lady. He had all sorts of objections but agreed to see her and when he did he was delighted as was the lady, though unknown to her I had to talk him out of clipping a pound or two off the wage. I argued she should receive the going rate — and she did.

Another success and one of much greater dimension came along when a pharmaceutical firm acquired a local former warehouse and had it restyled with a view to using it as their store from which to distribute their products to the north of England, Scotland, Northern Ireland and the northern counties of the Republic. The total labour force was to be just over one hundred.

When the manager arrived to take control he turned out to be a Lancastrian called Billings. We were to become good friends and good business associates.

Before coming north Billings had used two Glasgow newspapers to advertise for staff. This had proved to be quite expensive. What was even more disconcerting was when on his first day a mail van arrived with four mail-bags full of replies to his advertisements. Going through them was a momentous and dreadfully time-consuming exercise.

I had seen his advertisements and had gone round to see him. We discussed his situation and eventually we agreed that he would aim to recruit half his staff from the respondents and take the other 50% or so from the folk my colleagues and I would send to him for interview. We further agreed that after six months we would review the situation and see which method of selection had provoked the greater wastage both voluntary and involuntary.

When Billings and I conducted that assessment, which occurred at the time of my own resignation, we found to his surprise and to my pleasure, if not quite delight, that our half had been the more reliable.

There was too a case which was both a success and a failure. This involved one of our Big Mill coterie, a man called Niven. When we first encountered him we were moderately impressed.

It then transpired that he had started attending some of the services of a small Evangelical church and to their credit the members of this church had provided him with a fairly presentable tweed suit, two shirts and matching ties, assorted underwear, a fine pair of brogue shoes, two pairs of stockings and a slightly stained raincoat.

After seeing him again and speaking to him at some length I suggested I should try to get him a job as a hut-man in a camp attached to a civil engineering site in the peninsula beyond Stranraer. He was not averse to the idea. He would be responsible for keeping the hut and the adjoining ablutions facilities clean.

We did the requisite paper work and the company agreed to take him. We gave him his travel warrants, wished him well and said good-bye. He never arrived at the camp whereas other recruits did. The company expressed its displeasure. Later we learned that poor Mr Niven had died on the train somewhere between Girvan and Stranraer.

Our total unemployment seemed to settle to a new plateau around 1,200. We had managed to find work for some thirty or so of the men from Rose's Homes. The staff recognised we would not get our total below a thousand, so we discussed the situation and settled for a compromise. We went to the restaurant for High Tea.

John Devine died of a heart attack in the winter of 63-64. He had been about to be promoted but then he was promoted to a much higher status.

Wee Wullie Broon

This story started for me on the day of Princess Diana's funeral.

My wife and I were due to join a party from Duns Scotus Church in the Gorbals and then travel with them, first to Edinburgh airport and then to a town on the Adriatic coast. We were due to have a week's holiday in Cattolica and then proceed to Assisi for a week of pilgrimage.

When we arrived at the church the coach which was to take us to Edinburgh had not yet arrived and when it did the driver would not let us board until he had completed his paper work and was ready to stack our cases in the luggage hold.

Suddenly, I was half-pushed up against the side of the bus and a face pressed into my face. To be fair, it was not an aggressive face. It was an interesting, lively, even a possibly compassionate face. Above all, it was very much a lived-in face which told you that the owner of the face had not had an easy, comfortable life; that he had been around and been places and seen things, aye, and had maybe done things outwith the experiences of most men.

Then the face spoke. First came a sort of growl and then words. "Ur you or no' Tam Carbery?" it demanded.

"Guilty as charged," I replied.

"Thought ye wur," said the face. "Ah wus in your class in the Primary in 1933. We wur in Mr Moffat's class and then we wur in Mr Heaney's class. Then you goat intae Bridie Kane's class but Ah didnae get intae that class and ye know wit? They wur right, so they wur. Ah couldnae huv lived in her class. But Ah remember you well, so Ah dae."

"What's your name?" I asked.

The face smiled and the body to which it was attached seemed to have taken a half-step backwards.

"Wullie Broon," he pronounced. "Wee Wullie Broon. When Ah wiz a wean ma granny used tae sing a wee song. 'Wee Wullie Broon, Wee Wullie Broon, the finest wean in Glesca toon.'"

"Where did you live, then?" I asked.

"Through ra pend," he replied, and I knew exactly what he meant and all that his declaration implied.

The ensuing two weeks in Italy provided ample evidence that William Brown was the most pleasant, congenial, helpful and humorous of men. He was not the man for profound and grave discussion on Theology or even on Church affairs but he was excellent company and had a string of Glasgow stories which gave rise to roars of appreciative laughter. He tended to hang about with his own coterie of men, most of them called Jimmy.

The following year we had a week in Rome, staying in a modest hotel very near St. Peter's.

William and the Jimmies did not take kindly to "le petit déjeuner" which was particularly "petit" and each morning they crossed the road to a café which gave them egg on toast and more toast if they wanted it — which they invariably did.

One morning on returning from the café William came up to me and asked what I was planning to do with my day. I in turn intimated that I was conforming in that my wife and I were sticking with the programme.

"No' me!" said our hero and went on to observe that he had found he had had a bit too much of the ecclesiastical. He went on to observe that he had been involved in the Anzio landings. That as evening fell they had been subjected to heavy mortar fire from the Germans. One had landed beside him and his mate. His friend had taken all the blast. He had been killed instantly. If it had not been for his friend, he reckoned, he would have been killed.

He went on: "Ah said efter it that if ever Ah wis back that wey Ah wid try tae find his grave, so Ah wid. So that's whit Ah'm gonnae dae ra day, like. Ah'm gonnae go tae Anzio and find that grave. It's ra least Ah kin dae, isnae it?"

I agreed. And with a smile and a nod he was off.

That night I learned that without a word of Italian he had got to the railway station on the other side of Rome; that he had caught his train to Anzio; that he had taken a taxi to the War Cemetery where he had reckoned someone would speak English and having found that official he had been directed to the appropriate area and had found his friend's grave.

I asked him how long he had spent in the cemetery. Just over an hour, he said. And what had he done?

"Ah knelt doon and said some prayers," he said.

"Then," he went on, "Ah looked at ra ither graves roon-aboot like and Ah could remember some o' ra names and could remember some o' ra faces, bit no' a' uv them, like. Then Ah went back tae ma pal's grave and said mair prayers. Then ah noticed that a grave aboot ten yards away hid a lot o' flooers while ma pal's grave hid nane, so ah took some aff the grave that hid loads and pit them oan ma mate's grave. Ah suppose in a way that wiz wrang bit no a' that wrang, wiz it?"

I gave him absolution by smile and took him to the bar for a well-deserved drink.

Over the next three or four years we returned to the Cattolica/Assisi run. Some years William was with us and sometimes he was not. I never learned what determined when he was present and when he was absent. What I do recall was that the cheery bunch of travellers was even cheerier when he was with us. His wit and humour and bubbly disposition were on these occasions ever present.

Very infrequently we would see him in Glasgow, at some re-union party or at a Sale of Work for church funds. Invariably on such occasions he would be laughing and joking, his pawky Glasgow humour rippling through him.

One summer we went back to Rome but he was not present and so did not repeat his Anzio expedition.

Then tragedy struck. One night when he was returning from an evening at his Regimental Club near Charing Cross he was walking along Caledonia Road. No doubt he should have been on the pavement rather than on the road surface. Whatever the reason, he was on the road. He was hit by a car and we were told by the police that when they attended the incident he was already dead.

Willie was unmarried. He had a girl-friend but she had slipped into premature dementia. She was in a home in Crookston and for years he had visited her twice a week. She did not know him but he sat for an hour or so on each visit and held her hand and spoke quietly to her.

His "family" consisted of diverse nephews, nieces, cousins and the like. The authorities reported his death to them. To their credit, they arranged for him to be buried from Duns Scotus Church. When they arrived for the Requiem they came expecting a very quiet, sparsely attended affair. They were pleasantly surprised to find that the church filled rapidly, that folk were standing three, four and five deep at the back and yet others outside but straining to hear the proceedings.

I learned later, though many already knew, that he spent three hours every morning delivering newspapers, rolls and milk to elderly and disabled householders in the multi-storey flats.

When we were standing around outside the church waiting for the cortège to form up, I heard a woman beside me say to her friend, "Ma man will be fair birlin' in his grave at me gaun tae a Catholic chapel. But Ah don't care. Ah couldnae lat that wee man go without saying thanks and piein ma respects like. An' in ony case if yon Lord could go tae the funeral o the other judge, like, Ah thought Ah could dae the same, so Ah could."

The funeral was impressive but my lasting memory of Wee Wullie Broon was of a last day in Cattolica. We were waiting for our bus and the foyer of the hotel was cluttered with suitcases. Then he appeared, found a place for his modest suitcase and put his jacket on top of it. "Ur you gaunny be here, Tam?" he asked and went on: "Ah'm gaun tae ra lavvy but keep your eye on that jacket like. Ah widnae want tae lose ma wallet. It's goat a pawn ticket fur a pair o shoelaces."

The Lass Frae Auchterarder

Cathie Jamieson was a girl from Auchterarder. Her childhood had been spent in what is known as the Lang Toon and she had gone to school there. Our story starts when she was 14 years old. She had left school at the end of June and was said to be considering employment as a counter assistant in the shop of a local baker.

Cathie was a clever girl. In the post-war situation she would probably have gone to secondary school but this was in the mid to late Thirties. But although she was clever she was not a happy young woman, a situation almost entirely attributable to her father. It was not that he was cruel or physically assaulted her. The heart of the matter was that he was an old grump. Truth to tell, there was no pleasing him: he often stopped her from singing as she went about the house. Complaining and criticising were his favourite occupations. He was most comfortable when he was being crabbit.

So it was that one day when the house was quiet she wrote two letters — one to the baker and the other to her mother, whereupon she packed a small case not much larger than an attaché case and set out for the bus which took her to Glasgow.

Some months earlier her close friend Bunty Baxter had left the town, gone to Glasgow and was now working as a housemaid in a large house in the Pollokshields district of the city.

When Cathy arrived in Glasgow she asked a policeman to advise her how to get to the Pollokshields address. He directed her to where she would find the appropriate tram-car and told her the appropriate fare. He even told her where to alight and how to get from the stop to the house where Bunty was located.

On reaching the address and having walked up the substantial drive she made the mistake of ringing the bell at the front door which was duly opened by a well-built lady with flour on her fore-arms. Cathie asked whether this was the house where Bunty worked. The lady confirmed that it was but then directed her to the back-door.

As she provided the tea and the scones the older lady explained that the house belonged to a couple called Laidlaw. The husband was qualified as both a lawyer and an accountant. He had a big office in town. Mrs Laidlaw ran the house and was responsible for all the domestic matters. In addition to the Glasgow house the Laidlaws had a second house, which was in Kilcreggan.

As she sipped her third cup of tea and munched her way though her third scone, Cathie learned that the housekeeper/cook was called Mrs Bremner and she was a widow from the war. She had a son but he stayed with his granny in the Townhead airt and was a student at the Tech.

Cathie explained that she had come to town in the hope that Bunty knew of another house that needed a maid, preferably one quite near where they were. Bunty shook her head; she knew of no such opening. But Mrs Bremner looked thoughtful. She observed that "Madam" was away in London with her husband who was on a business trip. They were returning to Glasgow by the overnight sleeper train and were due back the following morning. She would speak to Madam at the first suitable opportunity. She explained that there had been a day girl called Sadie who had worked part-time but she had left and had never been replaced and she went on to observe that the house had fourteen rooms and all in all it was "ower much" for her and Bunty.

The following morning Mrs Laidlaw returned to take command of her home.

As the grandfather clock in the hallway was striking ten, a taxi rolled up the big drive and the lady of the house alighted. The taxi driver carried her two cases to the top where Mrs Bremner, who had been hovering in anticipation of the return, took command of them. As she did so her employer explained that the train had been running late; that she and her husband had gone to Central Station Hotel for breakfast where after he had seen her and her two cases into a taxi he had proceeded to his office. She went on to say that she was somewhat fatigued and that she would go up and rest, maybe sleep, until nearly one o'clock when Mrs Bremner should first waken her and then bring up a tray with a very light lunch.

The overall result was that it was well into the afternoon before the house-keeper found a time when she considered it an opportune moment to raise the matter of Cathie and her possible deployment in the affairs of the house. When she did so it soon because apparent that her timing could not have been better.

The result was that at about four in the afternoon Cathie was directed to go up to see Mrs Laidlaw and be considered for employment.

The interview went well and Cathie was told to stay but although the house was large, she would have to share a room with Bunty.

As the early months slipped by Mrs Laidlaw came to realise that Cathie was exceptionally good at needlework and was able to make all sorts of alterations and wee adjustments to the employer's wardrobe - so much so that she started taking Cathie with her when she and her husband were going to Edinburgh and even London. On one occasion Cathie went with the couple to Paris and on another to Zurich, though she did not actually travel with them. On the contrary, she travelled Third Class.

It is here that our story takes a dramatic turn.

When Cathie was in her late teens and had been in her post for just over four years, she was 'going out' with a local policeman, a handsome young sergeant. He generally took her to the cinema but occasionally they would go dancing at the Albert dance hall in Bath Street. It was coming round to the time when the Pollokshields Domestic Servants' Association was due to hold its Annual Ball in the prestigious and handy Plaza ballroom at Eglinton Toll. With this in mind, Cathie had been 'saving up' and had brought tickets with a view to asking her sergeant to the grand event.

And then it all went wrong!

Bunty had been sent to do some shopping and had returned with the shattering news that there were strong rumours circulating contending that the supposedly gallant sergeant was seeing at least two other girls in the area and worse, was already committed to going to the Plaza Ball with a girl from a house in an adjoining avenue.

Cathie was shattered, though Mrs Bremner observed that as she saw it, Cathie's pride was dented more than her affections.

Later that week a delivery boy arrived from a book shop in the centre of town. He had four books for Mrs Laidlaw and he had to see her as she had to ascertain the books were those she had ordered and, given that they were she had to sign for them. Mrs Bremner explained that the lady of the house had a visitor, a friend from the Sherbrooke Church, and was not be disturbed.

Mrs Bremner proceeded to explain to the boy that he would have to wait but went on to suggest to him that as he waited he should have a glass of milk and a slice or two of bread and jam. For his part the boy said that would be nice and he would like that very much. It was not without significance that the house-keeper gave the lad a very large glass and cut him two thick slices of bread, heaping one with home-made strawberry jam and the other with an even bigger portion of blackcurrant jam.

As the boy embarked on the impressive snack, Mrs Bremner observed he could have another slice with plum jam if he fancied that as well, and the lad, with a nod and a smile, indicated that would be fine.

Mrs Bremner embarked on quizzing him.

How old was he?

Fifteen, but he would soon be sixteen.

Did he like the job in the bookshop?

It was alright but he would soon be leaving as his father had arranged for him to serve an apprenticeship as a fitter with a firm in Kinning Park.

How did he spend his spare time?

He was in the B.B. and sometimes he went to the pictures and now and again to the dancing. At that point Mrs Bremner smiled a very broad smile.

Did he have a girlfriend?

"No' yet," he replied.

Bunty then looked in to say that the mistress would see him now so he lifted the bundle of books and followed Bunty out of the kitchen.

As soon as the lad was out of the room, Mrs Bremner nodded after him and suggested to Cathie that she should ask him to the "do" in the Plaza. Cathie's immediate reply was to protest that the boy was much too young, a valid objection which the older lady countered by observing that everybody grows older and much too quickly at that.

The charge and counter charges continued but before the boy came back to go out of the back door, Cathie had mentally succumbed.

So she asked the lad to accompany her as her partner to the Plaza Ball. The boy agreed. A friendship grew into a courtship and when he was 23 and she was 26 they were married at a Registry Office.

By the time of their marriage and of the ensuing honeymoon in Rothesay, the age difference was of no significance.

Then again, the boy-with-the-books, the-boy-of-the-milk, bread and jam had proved to be a most apt and able fitter. In addition, he had developed a rapport with the internal combustion engine and the other features of the engines of both motor cars and motor-bikes.

Furthermore, he proved venturous and set up his own business in a small workshop in Side Street near Eglinton Toll – and the Plaza Ballroom.

It is here that our story takes a rather mundane turn. It would have been pleasant had I been able to report that the small repair and maintenance business prospered and grew and grew; that the couple, Cathie and her husband, bought a house in Pollokshields and that the house they acquired was the former Laidlaw place, the house in which Cathie had worked and, indeed, where they had met.

But it was not so. True, the business did well, but it did not suit the owner to aspire to the dizzy heights of entrepreneurial activity. So the business remained small and the couple and their two children lived happily and contentedly in a tenement flat in Govanhill.

And yet and yet... there was to be one quite dramatic and certainly pleasant twist to our story. When Cathie had been in service, she was prone to singing as she went about her duties. There was no sign of this attribute in either of their two children. But it appeared and blossomed in a grand-daughter who, after training at the Royal Academy of Music and Drama, went off to sing with Scottish Opera, from time to time in leading roles. She had – she still has – a wonderful voice. Occasionally she is asked where she got her delightful voice. She smiles and says it was and is "a gift from God".

She is, of course, quite correct. But God sent it to Cathie – the lass frae Auchterarder.

1729

This story is an old story. It is not quite as old as the hills but it has been around since the inter-war years of the 20th century.

It is told again and again. Yet that said, it is not told everywhere. It is told mainly in University Mathematics Departments and elsewhere by mathematicians at dinner parties, in golf club houses and trains.

It appears that in those inter-war years there was an Indian railway clerk who was not merely a good mathematician, he was extremely good: indeed, he was brilliant at arithmetic. It was reported that his railway duties were not unduly onerous and that he spent much of his days filling jotters with more and more complicated arithmetical exercises. His name was Ramanujan.

As reports of his activities spread further and further and articles about him, articles invariably commending his ability and his zeal, started appearing in Indian newspapers, not least English-language papers, he became quite famous. People, particularly important and well-placed individuals, wrote to British broadsheets and journals arguing that elements in the UK should be taking greater cognizance of this remarkable man and deploy him to his advantage and that of British academia and possibly the UK economy.

When this was at its height one individual wrote a very compelling letter to the Maths Department at Cambridge, which Department was seen as the best of its kind in the country.

It was then that the Cambridge team of mathematicians made two errors. Firstly, they gave serious time to the issue, discussing it at length. Secondly, they decided to invite Ramanujan to join them. As to why that was an error will soon become apparent.

I have heard it said that when he arrived at Cambridge he was wearing his Indian clothing and carrying his pots and pans for ritual cooking. So far as the clothing was concerned, members of the Department had to give him much more suitable clothing, not all of which fitted him. Meanwhile, the cooking constituted an even bigger problem. Boarding house landladies kept inviting him to leave as cooking in rooms was *verboten* and the smells of the cooking permeated the house.

Such difficulties extended to the social events to which he was invited. He did not drink alcohol – not even British sherry. In addition, he was totally devoid of small talk.

All this was bad enough but the heart of the matter gave rise to the eventual, the inevitable outcome. Sadly, there was little scope for using him – other, that is, than to allow him to complete even more jotters. Moreover, he was unsuitable for lecturing and had no experience thereof. By the same token he was not very good at conducting tutorials.

All in all, things started badly and degenerated from there. So it was that it became more and more apparent that they had made a dreadful mistake. He had to go!

But how to get rid of him? Then, as they deliberated, they experienced a God-send, if any God-given situation can be said of something unfortunate. Ramanujan was diagnosed as having tuberculosis, whereupon a severance payment was created and he was bundled back to India.

Some months later it became known that the great Hardy, the head of the Department, had been invited to visit India, give some guest lectures and receive a healthy plurality of Honorary Degrees. Someone, on learning of his itinerary, suggested Hardy must visit poor Ramanujan in his sanatorium.

It was soon clear that this did not appeal one wee bit to the about-to-be decorated Hardy.

Nevertheless others pressed for a visit – however short. Furthermore, it was argued that if the press got wind of Hardy being within some twenty or thirty miles of the bedridden former colleague and yet did not go to see him, Hardy and the Department would be depicted as ogres. So Hardy capitulated. Someone quoted Aquinas in saying: "There is no such question as 'why do I do my duty?'"

Come the day Hardy's taxi drew up at the sanatorium. He was not impressed by what he saw; on the contrary, what he saw fortified his forebodings. That was bad enough but when he walked into the ward he was appalled.

There were 60 men, each man covered by a thin, ostensibly white sheet. The beds seemed very close together and by each bed was a shelf with a bottle-like glass dish for the spit from the consumptives.

He found Ramanujan's bed and barely recognised the ravished man in the bed.

"How are you, old man?" he asked.

"Very well," started the lying reply. "They treat me very well, yes, very well."

A longish silence ensued. Then Hardy spoke again.

"I'm sorry to report that the taxi which brought me here had a most undistinguished number."

"What was it?" Ramanujan asked.

"1729," replied Hardy.

By way of reply the body stirred and Ramanujan raised three fingers by way of partial protest, partial rebuke.

"Oh no," said the near-corpse. "It is the lowest number to be the sum of two cubes in two different ways."

And, of course, he was correct.

The Lonely Mr Alfred Tait

As I remember it, virtually all the adults in our little scheme, area, district – call it what you will – approved of and liked Mr Tait. Most of the ladies would refer to him as "that nice Mr Tait." Some adventurous souls would say "that awful nice Mr Tait." 'Awful nice' had always struck me as dreadfully contradictory but in Glasgow idiomatic speech we knew it was high commendation.

I can recall that as a boy of 11 or 12, I was rebuked by a very fine teacher of English for using the word 'nice.' "Lose it," he advised. "It is a lazy adjective and lacks precision. Do try to be more imaginative, more adventurous." He would scoff at those who would talk about a nice young man who had a nice girl friend, who was one in a nice family, who lived in a very nice house, in a nice street, in a nice part of town and who went on holiday, to a nice hotel in Scarborough, which was a very nice resort.

But the adults of our area or district had not sat at the feet of my teacher of English, and so it was that Mr Tait was acclaimed – and approved – as being nice, awffy nice and very nice.

Our story begins about 1950, about five years after the war ended.

Mr Tait, Mr Alfred Tait, lived alone in a three-apartment house in Bennan Square. He was a foreman in Niven's, a small to medium-sized engineering works in Jessie Street in Polmadie. His wife had died of cancer in 1946. He had two daughters of whom he was immensely proud, but both were married and lived rather far away – in one case very far away.

Both his girls had been in the Forces. The older girl had been an officer in the Wrens and had married a naval officer who, prior to enlisting, had been a solicitor. They now lived in Buckinghamshire. The younger girl had been in the Waafs in which she too had been commissioned. She had married a bomb-aimer in a 'flying fortress,' the name given to the B29 bombers used by the Americans for their day-light bombing of Germany – shades of the film "The Memphis Belle." The American husband came from Oregon and they were living there. Both the girls wrote regularly and phoned occasionally, but Mr Tait had a lonely existence.

And then he met and married Sadie Palmer. Both were members of the McCutcheon Memorial Church. One Sunday there had been ice on the roads and pavement. Sadie had grabbed his arm and acclaimed: "Oh Mr Tait, it's awffy icey. Is it a' right to take your airm?" and without waiting for an answer propelled him towards Calder Street, where she lived with a sister and an elderly mother.

One thing led to another. News of the "courtship" filtered through. They had been seen on a bus going into town to "the pictures." On a holiday Monday they had been seen in Ayr. Old Mrs Palmer had been in the Victoria Infirmary and Alfred had been seen with Sadie visiting the patient.

They were married in the McCutcheon Memorial and the ladies of the district had "speired" that the honeymoon had been in St. Andrews.

Virtually no-one had a good word to say about Sadie. Most of her critics were vague. "Ah just canny staun' that Sadie Palmer." "There's something about her gives me the creeps." "Sadie Palmer? Sadie Palmer is a scunner, a right scunner, so she is."

There were some who were more explicit. From them I inferred that virtually no-one liked Sadie. She was the antithesis of congenial. She was a dreadful gossip and was always critical of others. She was very prone to fault-finding.

The recurring query was: "What did that nice Mr Tait see in that dreadful Sadie Palmer?"

One lady was heard to say: "We are told that love is blind but surely to God he saw some of her shortcomings."

Katie Conroy who lived with a married sister and who "did a spot of cleaning" in diverse houses, did the Taits' house two mornings each week. Sad to relate, she was indiscreet. To be specific, she "reported" two incidents she had over-heard.

On the first of the two mornings the couple had been having breakfast.

"We are running out of marmalade, dear," said Alfie. Sadie rounded on him. "I don't need you to tell me what we need. I am perfectly capable of running this house. I have been doing it for some time now."

Six weeks later Katie heard another encounter over breakfast. Sadie got up from the table and rummaged in a cupboard. "You might have told we are short of marmalade," she protested. Alfie started to reply but was cut off. "There is no point in excusing yourself. I cannot be expected to handle everything."

One night in their bowling club, Alfred was heard to say to his friend John Conroy: "Oh, John, I crave for a little affection. I would love to have a cuddle but cuddles are not forthcoming."

Within two or three months of the marriage some or all this disaffection had been discerned. In company, Sadie was never known to call him "dear." One day in winter she was seen to take his arm. The cynics said that was more a safety precaution. It was a gesture of safety rather than of approval.

Sadie was said to have told a neighbour: "I don't believe in all than "luvvie-dovey" stuff. It's soft and unbecoming. It is unseemly."

John Conroy went on record as saying he was convinced the marriage had never been consummated.

Mr Tait died. He had a heart attack and died three days later. Mr Conroy said our friend had died "of a surfeit of misery."

At the reception after the funeral a lady who had worked alongside Sadie was bold and rude enough to ask: "Sadie, you clearly never loved him. Why did you marry him?"

Sadie was not put out, replying: "My brother-in-law told me that Niven's had the best widows' pension plan of all the work-shops in the south-side."

Unabashed, she smiled at her former colleague. "Have a salmon sandwich," she urged, and went on: "They ur awffy nice, so they ur."

Shawfield and the Rules of the Market

As I recall it, it was Sir Alex Cairncross, one-time Professor of Economics at the University of Glasgow, author of a very fine textbook on that devilish discipline and later Chief Economic Adviser to the Treasury, who argued he could teach the business community all the Economics they needed, by telling them three essential things and doing so in an hour – or less. The first and the most important of his three points was that of the determination of the price by the scissor-like interaction of Supply and Demand.

My favourite illustration of this dictum occurred one fine evening in June at Shawfield Stadium in, well, mainly in Glasgow.

Shawfield was for many years a twin-purpose stadium. It was the home ground for Clyde FC which in the inter-war years, through the hostilities to the post-war years, was a senior Scottish club which while seen as small-time stuff when compared to the two dominant Glasgow clubs could from time to time punch above its weight and, for example, win the Scottish Cup.

It was also used for dog, i.e. greyhound, racing and for the legitimate gambling which accompanies that supposedly sporting activity.

This dual purpose was not the only quirky aspect of this stadium. Approximately two-thirds of the site lay within the bounds of the City of Glasgow while the residual third was in Rutherglen and consequently in the County of Lanarkshire. I recall being told when I was a boy that it was Glasgow police who were assigned to the large part of the ground while their Lanarkshire colleagues attended to the smaller and more easterly part.

There was another aspect of the situation in that the ground was very popular with Junior football clubs for the playing of semifinals and finals of their rather numerous cup competitions. Such games in the years after the War could attract crowds approaching twenty thousand. The events I witnessed took place on one such early summer evening.

For the life of me I cannot remember which teams were playing. What I do recall is that it was a 6.30 p.m. kick-off and that the crowd was even larger than had been expected.

The attendance at such Junior Cup games tended to come from three distinguishable elements, each accounting for a rough third of the total. The first two thirds were made up of supporters of each of the two teams while the residual third consisted of neutrals and others who rolled along to see what should prove to be a boisterous, towsy game which could go either way.

The highest common denominator was that except for the retired, the recuperative and those who lived locally everyone else was coming from his place of employment so that hunger was another factor which loomed large. The overall result was that there were more food vendors than usual.

There were of course vendors at any game with the likelihood of a reasonable attendance.

'PK chewing gum, a penny ra packet!' could be heard at any game as could '*Times*, *News* and *Citizen*' from those selling newspapers. On the night in question these were joined by others offering food. 'Duncan's Hazelnut, tuppence the bar' was one cry. 'Cauld pies, tuppence a time' was another. 'Here's ra home-made macaroon bars' was a third.

Our about-to-be saddened hero had at least been innovatory; he was selling apples, but it soon became clear that he had never read the textbook by, or sat at the feet of, Alex Cairncross.

When he started he was confident and had put aside, temporarily as was to be revealed, the depth of his Glasgow accent.

"Here you are, folks," he cried. "Two for a shilling, the lovely eating apples. Sixpence a time, the lovely apples. A tanner for an apple."

He had few takers. As the kick off approached and the latecomers arrived he altered his pitch.

"Here you are – fourpence each, the lovely eating apples. Three for a shilling the lovely eating apples."

The game started promptly, yet as the first half progressed I could hear him still urging purchase, but with a further drop in price. His despair brought about a change in the accent and the use of English.

"Here youse are, folks. Four fur a shilling, ra lovely eating apples. Threepence a time, the lovely apples. Is that no' a great bargain, so it is!"

Shortly after half time I could hear him yet again.

"Here youse ur! Tuppence a time, the lovely apples. Six fur a shilling, the lovely eating apples."

The game ended. One set of fans was delighted. The other faction looked glum.

As we shuffled our way through the now open gates I could hear a despairing voice cry:

"Here you are, lads. A penny a time, the lovely eating apples. Twelve for a shillin', the lovely apples. Take them hame for ra weans."

But neither he nor his potential customers had bags in which to carry them home. I hoped he learned from his miscalculations. He adjusted his prices but he was too late. Sad!

What is in a Name?
Baltasar Neglected

Although this is a rather brief story, it reveals, albeit indirectly, a fault-line which runs through Scottish society and which, from time to time, bursts through and allows ready recognition. All too many Scots, however, choose to adopt self-imposed myopia so that they do not have to acknowledge what prevails.

To my regret I do not remember some of the details, though I do recall, with startling clarity, the main confrontation.

It happened in Edinburgh sometime in the late Fifties. I had been sent through from Glasgow to work in a sub-section of the Staffing Department of our Department's Scottish HQ. My task was to write the first draft of an internal paper on the likelihood of the various trade unions represented in the labour force in Scotland having recourse to industrial action. I remember thinking that this task should have been given to someone in our Industrial Relations section and I remember learning later that, somewhat ironically, that section was inundated with strikes. Someone recalled hearing of my regular attendance at Trade Union Weekend Schools and it was this that resulted in my secondment.

One day a man one grade above mine, a man called Dobbie, came into the extended broom cupboard which was my 'office'. Without engaging in social exchange he went straight to the point.

"Carbery," he pronounced, "I am told you are well informed on a wide range of Church matters, as well as Trade Unions. A strange mixture, I would have thought."

"Anyway," he raced on, "what I want to know is whether there is a Roman Catholic plot to take over the Civil Service. Is there such a plot afoot?"

He was clearly of a mind to prattle on so I forced my way into his concerns.

"Mr Dobbie," I said, "I would make two observations. Firstly, I am unaware of any such conspiracy. Secondly, I would think it most unlikely. Why do you ask?"

"Why do I ask?" he spluttered. "Why do I ask? This is why, this is why I ask," he half-roared, waving some sheets of paper.

"This is why I ask," he continued. "This is the list from the Civil Service Commission of the new Clerical Assistants assigned to us here in Scotland. It is the people who passed the examination. It is cluttered with Irish-Catholic names. So much so, they account for nearly 30% of the total."

"Mr Dobbie," I ventured, "I do not see how 30% constitutes a take-over bid."

"Oh, you don't, do you!" replied Dobbie.

"Mr Dobbie," I said, "I would suggest to you that were you to look at the matter more objectively you would not be so concerned and would not be as distressed as you appear to be now."

I stayed with it. "Let me put this to you, sir. If individuals are denied employment by most banks and building and insurance society offices and a whole range of firms in the private sector, then in a full employment economy, they are destined to be over-represented in the public sector, especially when entry is by open examination."

"You mean there is nothing we can do about it?" he almost spluttered.

"Mr Dobbie," I replied, "if the Commission has accepted them and assigned them to us, then that would appear to be conclusive. You could write to the Controller with your conspiracy theory but I fear it would not enhance your career prospects. *Au contraire*: I reckon it would impair, seriously impair, them."

Mr Dobbie snorted, but it was a snort of reluctant and highly regretted defeat.

Then he rallied.

"Well," he went on, "listen to some of the names." He consulted his sheets and read aloud.

Theresa Connaghan

John Joseph McMahon

Augustine O'Rourke
Anastasia Quigley
Bernadette Roarty
Patrick Joseph Sweeney
Daniel Michael Tracey

Then he snorted again. This time there was an element of disgust in the snort. Then he returned to the fray.

"What is this?" he growled. "Do you know how they pronounce this? Do you know?" And with this query thrown at me he jabbed a finger at one entry which read:

Naoimh Keough

"Yes," I said, "NEEV KYO would be a reasonably correct pronunciation."

It was clear Mr Dobbie was very angry, very upset.

"Why can't they have sensible, easily pronounced names – like Scottish names, like 'Cameron' and 'Gordon' and 'Stuart'? Why can't they do that?" he asked.

"Yes. I know what you mean", I said with insincere sympathy. "You have in mind names like:

Colqhoun
Dalziel
and
Menzies.

I had given them all the Edinburgh pronunciation of each and not the more common Glasgow pronunciation.

Dobbie spluttered. "They warned me about you. You are cheeky and rude and have no respect for your seniors and betters."

"I concede," I answered, "that is a not unreasonable assessment, Mr Dobbie. I accept the bit about seniors but not about betters. The two are not always synonymous."

Thereupon he spluttered yet again and departed. Significantly he never returned.

Initially, I felt pleased with myself. Truth to tell, I was in danger of being smug.

Then I realised that I had not succeeded. Indeed, I had forgotten the wise observation of Baltasar Gracián, the 17th century Jesuit who observed: "There is no such thing as a victory over a superior."

An Encounter in Gloucester Road

When I was a schoolboy, a small schoolboy, my Uncle Jim used to take me out on Saturday afternoons. Sometimes we went to a football match. Sometimes we would go to a cinema and sometimes we would go into the centre of town when he would buy me two or three small toy soldiers from Woolworths.

All our expeditions concluded with our returning to my grandmother's house where the unmarried Jim lived with his mother and two unmarried sisters. Invariably the radio was on. We would listen to *Sports Report* with the football results. That programme was followed by *In Town Tonight*, a programme based on interviews of differing length with personalities reported as visiting London. This programme was introduced by a recording of an orchestra (or was it merely a band?) playing the *Knightsbidge March* from the *London Suite* by Eric Coats.

Little did I know then that London and Knightsbridge in particular were to have a strong impact on my life.

I started my active service in the RAF by reporting to Lord's Cricket Ground and living in what had been built as luxury flats on the Prince Albert Road at the north side of Regent's Park. After my release from the Forces I was on the Editorial Board of a Co-operative Youth magazine and that took me to Buckingham Street, where Pepys lived and where all the streets came from the name of the one-time owner of the land – Francis Villiers, Duke of Buckingham. Remarkably there is an 'Of Lane'.

Later in the fifties and sixties I took three degrees from the University of London which not only took me to the massive Senate House, but to the bookshops, particularly the one diagonally across from Birkbeck College. My studies took me also to Bloomsbury and the British Museum and to the LSE.

Much later, as the century was rolling over, I returned to Russell Square and a small American university with which I did some work.

Different Government Committees saw me in other locations. The Broadcasting Complaints Commission was south of the river, diagonally across from the Palace of Westminster, while a Royal Commission on Gambling, chaired by Victor Rothschild, saw us just north of Berkeley Square.

There were, too, visits to MPs and peers which took me to Westminster, while membership of the Press Council as it then was took me to Blackfriars and Fleet Street at its busiest time.

But the decade which really tied me – almost married me – to London was the seventies.

From January 1970 until August/September 1979 I was the Scottish member of the original Independent Television Authority which, after commercial radio was added to our remit, became the Independent Broadcasting Authority.

Our eight-storey building was across Brompton Road from Harrods. This was Knightsbridge with the Hyde Park Hotel and Sloane Street with its Sloane Rangers. As I recall it, membership of the broadcasting body involved spending alternate Thursdays in London.

Occasionally I would stay at the Basil Hotel in Basil Street – well worth a story of its own. My Celtic colleagues from Wales and Northern Ireland regarded the Basil as too twee, so usually I stayed with them in a hotel along the Brompton Road, past the parish church and the Oratory, by the museums and the Scout HQ, towards the area around Gloucester Road.

In his *Rumpole* series, John Mortimer has Horace, his hero, and Hilda his wife living in a luxury flat in the Gloucester Road, though one is left to infer that the luxury has evaporated since the flats were built and the selling agent's flamboyant, confident and boastful brochure was available.

Nevertheless, Mortimer is wise. Were I to live in London it is to Gloucester Road that I would aspire – particularly the run from the tube station across the Brompton Road and northwest towards Hyde Park. All that and with the area to the east peppered with embassies and unfamiliar flags. For me Gloucester Road is London.

The other element in this story is from the University of Strathclyde. Conceived in 1963, Strathclyde was born in 1964. It proved to be more imaginative, more virtuous, less pretentious, less hide-bound and fettered than some, most – all? – of its sister universities.

One example of this related to a Post-Graduate Diploma course in Office Studies and Business Administration. For this course the university recruited students, mainly but not exclusively female, with a very wide assortment of first degrees. These first degrees were mainly in Arts but there were Science and other traditional university subjects. Prior qualifications in Music, Nursing, Divinity, Librarianship, Nautical Studies and even Medicine and Dentistry also made an appearance.

The students, originally twenty-four and at the end 120, each year were given a grounding in office skills and Business Administration and in Accountancy. Traditional academics tended to scoff at this course and readily poured scorn on it and all involved with it. Employers on the other hand loved it.

The Home Office, the Foreign Office and the Treasury regularly, annually, sent recruiting teams to Glasgow, specifically to interview those from the course who were interested in such Civil Service posts.

The BBC did the same, as did Unilever, ICI and two major newspaper groups. London Weekend and Thames TV came occasionally. The overall result was there was no graduate unemployment from that course. Even our failures were snapped up by eager employers.

One morning in glorious spring I was in Gloucester Road making for a fine bookshop with attractively-priced remaindered books when a very attractive and exceptionally well-dressed young lady approached. She smiled. I lifted my hat. "Strathclyde?" I ventured. The young lady acknowledged the accuracy of my query. She went on to ask kindly after various members of staff. From time to time I asked what she was doing now. These enquiries she side-stepped beautifully. She explained it was her boss's birthday. She and some colleagues always gave him chocolate cake to mark the occasion. She had been to a pâtisserie near my bookshop to collect it. Yet again I asked about her activities, and again she dodged my question and returned to asking after staff members.

Eventually she indicated she should be moving along. Once more I asked what she was doing. She smiled a most gracious, almost pitying smile.

"Let's put it this way," she said, "I'm the nearest thing to Miss Moneypenny you are ever likely to meet."

And with that she smiled again, said goodbye and went on her way.

Miss Preston of Preston

Miss Phyllis Preston of Preston radiated, epitomised Preston. She was born in Preston within a twelve month of the end of the First World War. She was raised in Preston and educated in Preston. She attended a good grammar school in Preston. When she was nearly eighteen she sat and passed the Civil Service Examination for Clerical Officers. She elected to enter the Ministry of Labour and was assigned to the employment exchange in Preston. Nevertheless, when she had done six months in that office, she was transferred to Penrith. When she had done two years in that office, her father, who had been in the Territorial Army, was back in the Army and her mother had "taken poorly." A letter from their General Practitioner was submitted to the Department and she was transferred to the Preston office.

In short, Miss Preston was back in Preston. Nothing dramatic happened until 1954. In that year she was put up for promotion. She was unsuccessful but in 1955 she was successful. Someone at Regional Headquarters decided that a change would do her a world of good. He made a few phone calls and Miss Preston, now a Grade 5 or Junior Executive Officer, was transferred to Glasgow.

The news that she was being sent to Glasgow did not exactly delight Phyllis. Truth to tell, she was dismayed and apprehensive. The Deputy Manager and Financial Officer was a Mr Doig, a Scot from Greenock. He assured her Glasgow was not too bad. He told her that St Mungo or Kentigern, who was the patron saint of the city, had given the place its name; that Glasgow meant "Dear Green Place"; and that Gorbals – until then a horror word for Phyllis – meant "the singing birds".

On the train north she revelled in travelling first class. The train was quiet and she chose a table for four and spread out a map of the city and its surroundings. She was impressed by the rural nomenclature of lots of the districts – Oatlands, Shawfield, Rutherglen, Burnside, Kings Park: there seemed, indeed, to be a lot of parks, particularly on the side south of the river. North of the river she found Maryhill, Lambhill, Possilpark, Springburn. All this augured well.

She started to feel quite content. She checked again the name of the Employment Exchange to which she was to report on the following day — Parkhead. She closed her eyes and saw a pleasant public park with well-cut lawns, abundant flower beds, flowering bushes and trees both coniferous and deciduous. At the end of her park was an extended village. This would be where her new location would be.

Reality shattered her. Parkhead Employment Exchange, she found at ten to nine the next morning, was at a busy intersection. An enormous factory — the locals referred to it as "ra Forge"— was surrounded by other noisy, dirty establishments. A "puggy train" ran across a road. It emitted dirty smoke. Her total impression was of noise and dirt.

The manager, a Mr Duguid, welcomed her warmly but did not refer to their location, the noise or the film of dust which lay on everything. She was told that he, Mr Duguid, had a different suit for every day of the week. Later her own observations confirmed this. Others assumed that the change of clothing was motivated by style or pride. She believed it was motivated by cleanliness.

Phyllis stayed in Glasgow and in Parkhead for just over three years. She was in good, warm, not inordinately expensive digs in Hillhead. She spent much of the dry weekends in the city's parks, some of which were outside the city itself. She was impressed by the very inexpensive public transport and found the city offered an excellent library service. It had eight theatres and an abundance of cinemas and dance halls, though she was too prim to go to dance halls on her own.

In the summer months she found British Rail ran cheap excursion fares to Clyde Coast towns, so she could grab a cup of tea and sandwich in the office and catch a train from town to Ayr, Troon, Largs, Gourock and Helensburgh.

She found that one of the advantages of Glasgow was that it was easy to get out of it. So it was that two things happened to Phyllis. Firstly, she adjusted to life in Glasgow though she was never reconciled to the noise and dirt of Parkhead which she regarded as a gross and unforgettable misnomer. Secondly, she learned to appreciate Preston all the more.

She worked her way back to an exchange in another Lancashire town. Later, much later, I heard she had been promoted to Grade 4 — Higher Executive Officer and that she was manager of a Grade 4 Employment Exchange in that same county.

I like to think it was Preston.

Holidays — in Bute

When I was three and four we had holidays in which my two parents and I travelled alone. In 1928 we went to Groomsport on the southern side of Belfast Lough where we stayed with Presbyterian relatives of my Belfast-born father. In 1929 we took a room in a wee house on the golf course at Southend on the Mull of Kintyre. The man of the house was a groundsman on the golf course. He was a friendly man who made a small golf club for me and extended his gift to include four golf balls.

It was a rather fundamental existence. When my mother enquired about toilet, lavatorial facilities, the lady of the house waved her hand over the fields and hedges and declared: "You can go where you like."

Each day we walked by a long path — and through a field with a bull in it — to a magnificent beach. As I recall it the weather held for that fortnight; had I been consulted, I would have voted always for a repeat of Southend. The absence of any lavatorial facility was the decisive factor — and so we went to Bute.

So in 1930 when I was five we had a holiday in Bute; and despite some misgivings we returned to repeat the experience in 1931 when I was six. This holiday of 1930 had been destined to be "different".

It was different in that my maternal grandmother, "Grandma Morrison", came with us. In fact, I suspect she paid for the holiday. Another difference was that the house which we used had been taken for a month, July, which of course included the Glasgow Fair Fortnight.

Most holidaymakers to Bute stayed in Rothesay. The house which we took was in Montfort, about three miles south of Rothesay. The accommodation consisted of the ground floor of a red sandstone terraced house in a cul-de-sac off the main road. On the other side of the main road there was a rocky area with pools of seawater and beyond that a dribble of sand. We had the Firth of Clyde with views across the water to Wemyss Bay, Skelmorlie and Largs and the northern end of the Island of Cumbrae.

The house at our disposal was the property of a doctor, a medical practitioner, who lived in Jordanhill in Glasgow. It was my mother who dealt with him, i.e. paid the rent or charge for the month's rent and collected the keys.

The accommodation at our disposal consisted of two rooms to the front, a second bedroom and a comfortable kitchen/dining area off which was a working kitchen-cum-utility room, with access to a bathroom of sorts, but with a flush toilet and Izal toilet paper. My mother and I used the bedroom to the front while the rear bedroom was taken by my grandmother.

There was a cupboard in the hall, located between the kitchen and the public room to the front, which was a horrid room with horsehair furniture and glass cases containing stuffed birds. It was a room we never used.

My father was not with us for the first fortnight but he did appear for the second fortnight. Moreover, my three aunts who lived with Grandma Morrison in Glasgow joined us for the weekend, particularly the long Glasgow Fair weekend in the middle of the month.

We used the house as a base. Quite frequently we would go by omnibus to Rothesay and then by tram to Ettrick Bay on the west side of the island. It had a great beach but it did not have the impressive rollers of Southend.

Another activity was to go to Kerrycroy, a beautiful village farther down the east coast, and, as we understood it, adjacent to the private estate of the Marquis of Bute. The Butes were a wealthy family who had made their money from their land in South Wales, not least their "Bute's Mile" where they raised considerable funding from the mining industry and the export of coal.

My mother was no great cook but I remember great picnics and evening meals, mainly salads and cold meats — not least potted hough — and "pieces" of bread, butter and strawberry jam, which came from triangular jam jars bought from a licensed grocer's shop on the front in Rothesay.

Here we reach the events that led to the decision not to return for a third holiday. When my mother first went over to Jordanhill, as much to be vetted by the doctor as well as to make the payment and uplift the keys, the doctor asked her whether she was trustworthy. She said she was. "Good," he had commented and then went on: "Here is the ring of keys for the house. As you see, there are four keys. The big heavy key and the Yale key are for the front door. The silver one is for the back door and that gives access to the drying green and there is a bench for sitting, should you choose to use it. The old key is for the cupboard in the hall. I really should take it off but that is hard and difficult and even more so to put it back on the ring. So I am leaving it on, but you haven't to use it. The contents of the cupboard are very precious and dear to me. So, as I say, do not use that key. Think of yourself as having three keys; the two for the front door and the one for the back door. As for the payment, I see you have brought cash. That is good. I find cheques are troublesome…"

My mother thought nothing of it.

In the course of the 1930 holiday there were to be three mornings when, over breakfast, my grandmother observed that her sleep had been disturbed: she had been wakened by a strange series of bouncing noises which intensified and then diminished. Both the adults were perplexed but eventually attributed the noise to the working of the hot water system.

Things came to a head during the 1931 holiday. In the course of the first fortnight my grandmother reported two further instances of the bouncing noise disturbing her. With less than a week of the holiday to run she heard it again. This time she rose from her bed, put on her dressing gown and reported to my mother, who stated, admitted or claimed that she too had heard a bouncing noise. It was significant, the ladies concluded, that the kitchen fire had not been used the preceding evening, a situation from which they concluded that, whatever the cause of the noise, it could not be attributed to the hot water system.

So it was my mother reached for the keys, took the old key for the cupboard and, ignoring the doctor's injunction, opened the cupboard. It was very dirty and almost empty. What it contained was a golf bag with some clubs and a solitary golf ball.

Rightly or wrongly they attributed the noise to the deployment of this equipment, though by whom or by what they just did not know. A few days later we returned to town.

My mother returned the keys, doing as she had done a year earlier. She thanked the doctor and reported we had all enjoyed and benefited from the holiday.

In 1932 we went to Girvan. In 1933 we went to Millport. In 1934 we went to Innellan. As a family we did not go back to Bute and certainly not to the red sandstone house at Montfort.

Epiphany

There are those who can find no humour in anything religious. They are, of course, mistaken – or myopic.

Rikki Fulton kept us going for years with his Reverend I. M. Jolly, and was it not he who introduced us to the quasi-bigot "Reverend Noah Timm"? Meanwhile, television series like *Father Ted* and *The Vicar of Dibley* were very successful, while at a more modest level the one-time Moderator of the General Assembly and former minister at Dornoch Cathedral, Dr Simpson, had a number of books on church humour.

This story concerns three characters – a girl of nine or ten, her teacher in a Church of England school in industrial Lancashire and their local Bishop.

The Bishop had called to inspect the school on Religious Instruction. After an affable-enough exchange with the teacher he turned and addressed the pupils.

"Well, now," he opened. "Who can tell me about Epiphany?"

A healthy plurality of hands were raised and His Lordship chose a girl in a bright cotton dress and cardigan. The girl took a step into the aisle, bobbed a sort of curtsy and proclaimed in a fine clear voice, albeit in the local accent:-

"If it pleases Your Lordship, Epiphany is porter at railway station when you're going to Blackpool at holiday time."

Total incredulity creased the face of the prelate.

"I beg your pardon. Could you repeat that?" he asked, and responding readily with another bob the girl repeated her answer. She was confident. She knew her stuff. Epiphany was the railway porter when you were going your holidays.

Totally confused and astounded, the Bishop turned to the young teacher.

"Did you teach them about the Epiphany?" he asked.

"Oh yes, my Lord," replied the teacher. "I covered it most thoroughly."

"Did you indeed?" said the ordained. "And what exactly did you say it was?"

"I told them it was a manifestation," she proclaimed proudly — and she too said it in the local accent.

Dr Pat Connolly

As I write, Dr Pat Connolly is 97 and, with the grace of God, will soon be 98.

Patrick was born in County Monaghan in the years prior to the First World War. In his late teens he came to Glasgow, to the University of that city — and at that time its only University. He studied medicine and duly qualified as a doctor. He was to prove to be an exceptionally good doctor and his diagnostic skills were (and are!) quite first class.

For many years he and his brother Eugene and a lady doctor, Maureen Aylmer, ran a very successful practice in Cathcart Road, near the Herman Baptist Church and across the main road from where Aikenhead Road comes to the T junction with Cathcart Road.

One remarkable aspect of his colourful and fascinating life was that he was a prisoner of the Japanese. Not many men who spent over three years in those dreadful camps have lived to within a sneeze and a cough of one hundred.

Our story, however, concerns the tranquil period prior to the Fall of Singapore. The Officers' Mess in that camp had an Indian man who was invariably referred to as 'That Indian Wallah'. That Indian Wallah was expected to work exceptionally long hours. He was expected to be behind the bar serving drinks till nearly two in the morning and to be up and about by 6.30 a.m. at the latest in case someone wanted an early breakfast. He never had a day off.

The outcome was inevitable: he died! The day after the death the Commanding Officer approached Pat. "Connolly," he opened, "I am told we cannot bury, burn or otherwise dispose of the Indian Wallah's body until I obtain a death certificate. Write one out for me, Connolly, there's a good chap!"

Pat did what was asked of him and attributed the death to 'Premature Old Age'.

That night the CO came storming into the Mess.

"Connolly," he roared, "I'm not having it. You young fellers cannot deceive me. Premature Old Age, indeed! I'm no medical man but I know that is not a disease. I'm not having it. Write me a proper death certificate and have it on my desk by nine o'clock tomorrow." And with that he tore up the original certificate and threw it into a waste paper basket.

Patrick did as he had been ordered. At 9.15 a.m. the CO came into the dining room where Pat was having breakfast.

"Thank you, Connolly," he opened, while waving the new certificate. "Much better, much, much better. Thank you."   And with that he wheeled away, to speak to the Adjutant.

Patrick had written: 'Cause of death — Disintegration'.

Dizzy Daisy Dickinson

They called themselves "Les Girls". There were ten of them. They were all graduates in diverse disciplines from a sweep of Scottish universities. They had met when, as post-graduate students, they had attended the great Jordanhill College of Education in Glasgow, a proud establishment and acknowledged as the largest and possibly the best teacher training college in Europe. Those who attended – be it for three years or for the one post-graduate year - were "branded". There was even a Jordanhill accent.

By the time of our story they were all qualified and competent teachers. They were all teaching, if not in Glasgow itself, then at least in the conurbation which had a population of just over two million.

During their Jordanhill year the friendship had formed. Affinity had been assisted by good organisation. There are those who contend that friendship should be left to grow, to develop naturally. But consider, if you would, the state of a garden which was left to grow naturally…

Throughout their Jordanhill year, the chats between lectures, over the plentiful cups of coffee both in College and in the cafés of the West End, the evenings in wine bars and the like, the friendship had been fortified, had been supplemented by an "organised" event on the evening of the last Friday of each month. So one month they would go to an upmarket restaurant for dinner, while in May they went to Ayr to walk along the promenade and later eat fish and chips. There was always something.

They had continued the practice but confined it to every second month. As the years rolled on modest affluence (and the acquisition of cars) opened the door to new and intriguing activities.

All that said, in terms of home addresses they fell into three sub-groups. Four of them lived in the West End, three were to the north outside the city boundary — one each in Bearsden, Milngavie and Lenzie — while the final three lived south of the river in Giffnock, Clarkston and Newton Mearns.

Daisy Dickinson was unmarried; it was she who lived in Giffnock. The other two southsiders arranged to collect her and take her to the hotel where they were to have lunch. When they arrived at Daisy's house, they were a little bit early. Dizzy was her usual not-quite-organised self. She was uncertain as to which of two handbags to take with her, a situation which had resulted in the total contents of one being transferred to the other, only to be switched back to the original bag.

Suddenly Dizzy shrieked and explained that she just had to change. Her two friends took this to refer to an item of clothing – her shoes, skirt or jacket. "I shall only be a minute or two," pronounced Daisy as she fled into her bedroom.

It was nearly twenty minutes before she reappeared. Her friends were only too aware that they would now be late for their lunch. To her credit when she did reappear Daisy was duly apologetic. "I'm sorry," she said. "That took longer than I thought."

Her two friends looked at each other. Nothing was said but by body language and glance they acknowledged that their annoyance at now running late had been superseded by perplexity. Daisy was wearing the same outfit as before. Had she switched her ensemble only to return to the original choice? After all, mused one later that day, she had returned to the original handbag.

It was as though Daisy had become conscious of their bewilderment.

"I remembered that I am going at four o'clock to Ross Hall (a private hospital) to see a doctor." And she raced on: "And my mother always told me to put on fresh underwear before going to a doctor. After all, as my mother said, you never know what the doctor might want to see. In fact, I had a quick shower as well."

"What kind of a doctor is it?" asked Janet McKinlay.

"A good doctor," said Daisy.

"No doubt," said Janet, "but what is his speciality? Is he a surgeon?"

"No," replied Daisy. "He's an ophthalmologist."

Daisy could not understand why the other two burst out laughing and why the other seven also roared with laughter when, eventually, they reached the hotel and joined the others and it was explained why they were late.

Just an Excuse

Once upon a time there were two West of Scotland Members of Parliament who were referred to by their Scottish colleagues and others in the wider Labour Movement as "Semmit and Drawers". This unbecoming nomenclature was bestowed on them as they seemed to be well-nigh inseparable. To be fair, each had a private life — a family, a home, friends and relatives. The nomenclature was ascribed because in their public lives they were always, or nearly always, seen together. They sat together on the Labour benches. They travelled together. They were both supporters of the whisky trade in Scotland. They took very similar stances on political issues and as a result they did not cause problems for the members of the Whips' Office. And they were very likeable.

Our story concerns two trade union leaders who were very like our two politicians, though their visible affinity did not give rise to either smart or rude nomenclature.

They were Danny Crawford and Donald McGregor who in their day were the secretary and president of a union, that of the Scottish Painters. As with the MPs, they went around together and you could not put a bus ticket between their views on Trade Union and political issues. The Labour Party leadership could rely on their support. They were the most congenial of men. I was always pleased to meet them — and of course when we did meet I invariably found the two of them together.

They ran their union very well, indeed one might say in an exemplary manner. It was therefore no surprise that they were re-elected year after year.

That said, I was somewhat surprised when I saw the voting figures. They each received a very substantial vote and readily saw off any foolhardy soul — generally of the Hard Left — who stood against them.

One day, I asked McGregor how they did it.

"It's easy," he said. "I attract the Masonic vote and Danny attracts the Catholic vote and we each tell our troops to vote for the two of us — and they do."

As our friendship deepened they engaged me to do weekend schools for them. A variant on that arrangement would occur when I was covering such a school for the T.U.C. Educational Service which in Scotland was run by a Communist who — to his credit — drew his tutors from across the whole arc of the movement's political spectrum. When Danny Crawford and Donald McGregor knew I was doing such a school, they would circulate their more enthusiastic members urging them to attend.

Then came the dramatic weekend school.

It started quite prosaically.

"Tom, could you do a weekend school for us over the last weekend of next month?"

I looked at my diary and indicated that I could do it.

"What is it to be on, what topic do you want me to cover?"

The reply surprised me. "Anything," they said, in unison. I said they had to be more specific and prattled along about pipers and tunes.

"Don't be difficult," said Danny Crawford. "Do it on whatever subject you believe appropriate."

Certainly they were being kind but I was for none of it, so I offered, nay declared, I would send them a postcard showing three possible topics. They were to score out two of them and return the card.

"You are fussing," pronounced Donald McGregor. He was peeved at my stubbornness but we parted on good terms.

I sent my postcard but it was slow in coming back to me. When it did, all three options were still there. Nothing had been deleted. So I went for the first of the three and advised then accordingly.

Come the day the School was in the Dunblane Hydro. There were to be three sessions: one before dinner on the Saturday evening and the other two on the Sunday morning on either side of the coffee break.

The Saturday session went very well. I could not have asked for more. There were nearly 200 delegates. The questions were good, the audience appreciative. On the way out some folk told me they had enjoyed it.

Sunday was rather different. I should have realised it when, at breakfast time, the dining room was quiet and nearly empty. When I started the first of the two morning sessions my audience crept into double figures – eleven to be precise, and that included a man who fell asleep during my introductory remarks. As the session proceeded (if such is the word) some others drifted in. By the coffee break there were eighteen in the body of the kirk. Over the coffee session there was no sign of either of our senior officers.

One thing did happen. The wee lady who was pouring the coffee observed she had never known such a high percentage of the requests being for black coffee. When we resumed, the attendance had soared to between thirty and forty. Again, some folk crept in sheepishly with the overall result that when I brought the School to a close and thanked them for their attendance there were sixty delegates clapping politely.

Over lunch I spotted them — together, of course! I had the impression they would have avoided me if it had been possible.

"What's gong on here?" I asked.

"What do you mean?" asked Danny.

So I told them, pouring my indignation over them.

Eventually they looked at each other.

"You tell him," they said, saying it simultaneously.

And so the story emerged. They were about to merge with, be taken over by, the Amalgamated Association of Woodworkers. They would see the merger through and then retire. But there was a very healthy Education Fund and they were not going to see it being taken over by the new English management. So they had the Weekend School and each delegate was on £20 a man, ostensibly expenses, but in truth drinking money. And the members being compliant had spent it at the bar on the Saturday night.

As for me — I had been the excuse for a booze-up.

The Woman in the Next Bed

This story is about a wee girl of eight or nine who was in hospital in Edinburgh.

I obtained the story from a delightful couple whom we meet every year in Puerto Pollensa in the north of Majorca. We meet them there; we never meet them in Glasgow or Edinburgh, though we do hear about them from another Edinburgh couple who know us and know those who related the tale. They meet at church, all four of them being members of the large Baptist Church at the West End of George Street.

The wee girl was not at all put out by being in hospital. She trusted the doctors and got on well with the nurses who made a bit of a fuss over her. The wee girl, however, was intrigued by the woman in the next bed. She had told the wee girl she was 34 but the child's mother reckoned 47 or 48 was nearer the truth. She had badly dyed hair and painted fingernails and toenails. She had mascara on her eyelids and badly applied lipstick. The nurses worked assiduously to remove such decoration but before each visiting time, when raucous ladies came to visit her, the facial enhancements re-appeared.

From time to time the woman would tell the wee girl that she was "stepping out" for a wee smoke or a wee hauf.

"Tell them Ah'm away tae the lavvy, hen," she would urge.

One evening the wee girl's mother came in alone to visit her daughter. The adjacent bed was empty. The latter-day Boadicea had slipped out for a wee smoke or a drink or both.

After the usual pleasantries and having ascertained that the child had no news of her own, the mother nodded her head in the direction of the temporarily empty bed.

"That lady, that woman," she corrected herself, "that person in the next bed, what is she in for, what is her ailment? Do you know?" The child looked thoughtful.

"I don't know, Mum," she said and then after a long pause added. "But I know she is a nun. I found out."

The mother immediately queried, indeed contradicted this observation.

"No, no, Ishbel. You must be wrong, dear. She is not a nun!"

"But she is a nun," the child persisted. "I know she is a nun. I found out."

"What do you mean, dear?" asked the now confused mother.

"Well," explained the child, "one day when she was away smoking I got out of bed and looked at her chart at the bottom of her bed. And do you know what it said, mum?"

"No, tell me."

"Religion — None."

Juxtaposition

In many ways it is unfortunate that the jibe at the heart of this story involved my friend Jim Craigen, who was for some time the Labour and Co-operative MP for Glasgow Maryhill. Jim is as straight as a Roman road. He radiates probity and rectitude. Had he still been in the House at the time of the Expenses Scandal, I am sure *The Daily Telegraph* would have found nothing untoward in his expenses.

This tale, however, occurred much earlier in his career when he was employed by the S.T.U.C. and was a member, an elected member, of the Corporation of the City of Glasgow. Shortly before the events of this story occurred he had been promoted to Bailie and thereupon became the youngest-ever Bailie in the history of the city.

By and large the members of the Corporation did a very good job but it was not unknown for someone to disappear from the benches of the Council Chamber and, after a brief appearance in the Sheriff Court, to proceed thereafter to the delights of Barlinnie Prison on the northeast side of town. In short, these unfortunates had foolishly succumbed to the temptations for easy money which went with the job of being a member of the Corporation.

The evening concerned was spent not in Glasgow but in St Andrews where we were attending the S.T.U.C. Summer School. It was an extremely pleasant evening, and some seven or eight of us were out strolling our way through the town. Jim was in the advance group while I was with the laggards.

Then I noticed a large, impressive shop, the front of which was decorated with pronouncements to the world and his wee brother that they had regularly provided their wares to the Queen, the

Queen Mother and the Prince of Wales. Further claims followed.

I hailed Jim across the intervening fifteen yards of pavement.

"Jim," I cried, "there's a statement on that shop which, with some paraphrasing, would do for some of your Corporation colleagues. They could stick it on the front of the City Chambers."

Somewhat confused, Jim intimated he was not with me.

"Look," I cried, "it reads 'Licensed to deal in Game'. Some of your lot could put up 'Game to deal in Licences'. The others laughed but Jim was not amused. To his great credit he never held it against me.

A Clean Sweep

The events of this story took place in the middle to late fifties of last century.

A new, wonderful carpet shampoo had come on the market. I believe it was made by the Bex Bissell Co, but I could be mistaken. There was not the slightest doubt about its success. When it appeared, the demand far outstripped the supply. This could have been a marketing ploy on the part of the manufacturers. Certainly there are firms which had recourse to this "restricted supply" tactic. I know of one popular liqueur whereby this tactic was used in the early days of the product's existence.

In the fifties young stenographers could be seen receiving private phone calls, then grabbing their coats and handbags and fleeing from the office, to be seen on their return some thirty minutes later, awkwardly grabbing and holding on to a large cardboard box, triumphantly declaring to the world that it, the cardboard box, contained a carpet shampoo.

Ready testimony was then forthcoming on how effective the shampoo had been and old carpets were said to shine and exhibit again their forgotten colours.

The shampoo, when obtainable, sold for 67/6, i.e. three pounds, seven shillings and sixpence.

This was a scenario, by all accounts, repeated again and again the length and breadth of the country. And then, in Glasgow, beyond the Hielandman's Umbrella there was a small department store, which store gave rise to a remarkable development.

With bravado the management of the store — I think it was called Inglis's — announced that henceforth they would sell the very shampoo, not at 67/6 and not even at 57/6 but at the ridiculously low price of 47/6.

As I recall it, the manufacturers were not amused. At that time resale price maintenance prevailed in Britain. That meant that goods had to be sold all over the country only at the price indicated by the firm which made the product. As I recollect it, the firm took the wee store to court, counsel arguing that the shampoo could not legally be sold for less than 67 shillings and sixpence. It was conceded that a wholesale price of 36 shillings and a retail price of 67 shillings and sixpence gave the retailer a very healthy profit, but, it was argued, the retailers had to be enticed by the abnormal profit of 31 shillings and sixpence on an outlay of 36 shillings — this being required as the boxes were big and bulky and took up considerable store space. Moreover, it was argued, even if the Court did not accept the inducement argument, the law clearly stated that the retail price had to be that decreed by the manufacturer. The manufacturers said 67 shillings and sixpence so 67 shillings and sixpence it had to be. The Court agreed. The manufacturers had won. Inglis and a price of 47/6 had lost.

So Inglis's had lost? Well, in one sense yes, but they were to prove to be resilient.

There are those in Marketing who declare that there is no such thing as bad publicity which cannot frequently be turned to one's advantage. Inglis's announced they would not sell the shampoos at 67 shillings and sixpence. What they would do was to give them away!

So they advertised that if a customer brought his or her old scrubbing brush, the store staff would swap it for a shampoo — a shampoo worth 67 shillings and sixpence. Inglis's had already received lots of good publicity as the almost philanthropic retailer who had been halted by the law. Now they received even more wonderful publicity and all free of charge.

Events then took another quirky, unforeseen turn. Tenants of ground floor flats in city centre tenements found that all scrubbing brushes left out on window ledges thereupon disappeared. Impecunious men, not least the residents of the model lodging house in Holm Street (between Argyle Street and St Vincent Street), purloined, appropriated, uplifted, confiscated, stole, pinched as many of the brushes as they could.

Having acquired the scrubbing brushes the thieves — for such they were — then went to the store and duly swapped the brushes for the boxed shampoos. This led to a series of dramatic scenes.

Ladies from Bearsden, Newton Mearns, Uplawmoor, Kilbarchan, Thorntonhall, Bothwell and the like — ladies who were inclined to wear fur coats in winter and silk lingerie in summer — were accosted in Sauchiehall Street, Gordon Street and Buchanan Street by smelly, dirty, unshaven men who hailed them with an affable query: "Hey, Missus, wid ye like to buy wan o' them great carpet shampoos? Ah'll gie you this wan for a quid, so Ah will." Many of the ladies sniffed and scurried on their way. But others produced single pound notes, which we had in those days, and so obtained their carpet shampoos — and then realised they had to trachle them home.

The main beneficiaries of this exercise were the men from the model and taxi drivers.

And, of course, Inglis's, who continued to receive not inconsiderable publicity. Sadly, that store has gone, but so too have many others of Glasgow's old-style department stores.

The Lord Helps Those Who Help Themselves

No doubt you have noticed that some folk are very good, very adroit at finding and then exploiting situations which advance their careers. This story is about such a man. Moreover, he was noted for it.

At the end of the First World War he was living with his wife and their clever daughter in Weston-super-Mare where he was employed as a minor official in the offices of the Local Authority.

He was a tall, handsome, good-looking man. He had, too, a good bearing; he carried himself well. If he had lived in Scotland where folk can be more outspoken, some frank, forthright neighbour on seeing him pass by would have remarked: "That chiel has a graun conceit o' hissel." And no-one in the house would have demurred.

In addition to his "municipal" duties he led an active life. He was the Vice President of the local Co-operative Society and was well-to-the-fore in the local Methodist Church where he was a lay preacher.

In the early twenties his daughter was due to sit a critical bursary examination. One evening over supper he told the girl that if she was successful he would give her a treat: he would take her to London for a day trip.

The daughter was successful and he, in turn, kept his promise. He and the daughter went to London. Significantly, the wife did not accompany them.

The trip to London was a great success. A good royalist, he started by taking her to Buckingham Palace, then through the park to the Palace of Westminster, with the Commons and the Lords. They then progressed up Whitehall with the Cenotaph, Downing Street and on the opposite side of Whitehall, New Scotland Yard and so to Trafalgar Square with the National Gallery and the Portrait

Gallery, St Martin's-in-the-Fields and the imposing buildings of the larger Commonwealth countries. After a brief lunch in The Strand they went to the Tower of London.

On the bus back from the Tower he read an item in the paper he had purchased. This referred to a Mr H. J. May who was the Secretary to the Co-operative Party, the political wing of the British Co-operative Movement. Mr H. J. May, it was reported, would soon be leaving his present post as he had just been appointed as Secretary of the International Co-operative Alliance at its HQ in Switzerland.

On reading this he advised the daughter they would alight at Trafalgar Square as there was a Post Office round the back of the church.

Once in the Post Office he consulted a telephone directory and ascertained the address of the Co-operative Party Office. As he had suspected, this was down off Victoria Street, not all that far away.

Courage never goes out of fashion, though what ensued was as much cheek and audacity as it was courage.

He and the girl then walked to the Party Office, where he explained to the young lady in the outer office that he wanted to see the Secretary.

On gaining entry to the inner sanctum he explained who he was and went on to say he was delighted to hear of May's new appointment and added his sincere congratulations. The secretary was kind and gracious and offered tea to his unexpected guests. It was over the tea that our hero raised the matter which was the real *raison d'être* of the visit.

"What would be the chances of my succeeding you in this post?" he asked.

It was learned later that Mr May was somewhat taken aback at such direct action, but went on to play it with a straight bat. The post would almost certainly be advertised. The advertisement would probably appear in both the national and the Co-operative press. Doubtless there would be many applicants and a selection would be invited to appear for interview. No doubt his visitor would apply. He did. So did 160 others.

Ten men — they were all men — were called for interview. He was one of the ten. In the course of his interview he made sure of stressing his interest in the post. An indication of this enthusiasm was his calling on the day of the news of the incumbent moving to Switzerland. On that occasion he had expressed not only his congratulations but his interests in succeeding to the London post.

"Is this correct?" asked the Chairman and in turn was assured that was what had occurred.

The interviewing panel was impressed by his appearance, his bearing, his confidence, his eloquence and, above all, his enthusiasm.

He was appointed as Secretary to the young, small but growing Co-operative Party.

A year or so after his appointment the Executive Committee of the Party was plodding its way through a routine meeting when a certain issue arose. It was noted that many individuals were being adopted as Parliamentary Candidates. The Executive Committee members found it wounding that they were not being considered. It was agreed that a letter should be sent to the branches saying that when the selection of possible MPs was before them branches should consider not merely local activists but those at national level – such as the Executive Committee of the Party.

"And its Secretary," suggested the Secretary.

"And its Secretary," echoed the Chairman.

And so the letter went to the branches.

Within a twelve month our hero found himself on a train travelling to Sheffield, a town about which he had known very little but about which by then he knew a great deal. He was to be interviewed as a possible prospective Labour and Co-operative candidate for a Sheffield constituency. When he took the train back to London he was the prospective candidate.

In 1924 Labour won the Election and our hero was not only elected, he was given minor office. He was a junior minister in the Admiralty. It did not last long. Labour was pushed out of office but he was still an MP.

In 1929 it happened again. Labour won and he returned to his junior office. Again, the Labour Government did not last long.

Through the hard days of Ramsay MacDonald and then Baldwin and eventually Chamberlain, Labour was a sad minority — but he was still an MP.

Then it all went right for him.

In 1940 Churchill usurped Chamberlain and set up a Coalition Government. On becoming Prime Minister Churchill's own post as First Lord of the Admiralty became vacant and who better to fill the shoes than a Labour (and Co-operative) man with experience of the Admiralty.

He never looked back.

He saw out the War in that post. In 1945 Labour won and formed its own government and he, of course, retained full ministerial office.

By the end of that Government in 1951 he had been Minister of Defence. He went to the Lords. The Royal Family had taken to him and he was a frequent guest at dinner parties.

He finished his days as Earl Alexander of Hillsborough, Companion of Honour.

The Foreign Correspondent

Dan Crampsey was the father of the three Crampsey boys – Robert, Frank and Philip – and of their two sisters, Julie and Catherine. As a young man Dan had left the family home in Carndonagh in the Inishowen peninsula. It is one of the quirky aspects of Irish life that the most northern part of Ireland is not in Northern Ireland. *Au contraire*: it is in the Republic. Mallinhead is at the top of Inishowen and the most northern town in Carndonagh.

As a young man he came to Glasgow, where he found a job in a bar. He was extremely careful with his money and in due course opened a public house of his own. It was down at the bottom of Shields Road, where that road meets Kinning Park and, good for trade, it was near Shields Road underground station.

By the time I got to know Dan, his family back home in Carndonagh consisted of a brother and a sister. The lady was a nurse and the brother, Willie, had a prosperous business of his own. It was a shop which was a newsagent's, a tobacconist's, a confectionery which also carried a small range of hardware items. Both Willie and his sister lived in a flat above the shop.

As I learned more about them I came to know that Willie saw himself as a correspondent, committed to keeping Daniel fully informed of all that was happening, not only in Carndonagh but in the northern half of the peninsula. As though that was not enough, he occasionally extended his report to the national political scene in Dublin.

All this he did by sending the local weekly newspaper, which he supplemented by writing along the margins of the inner pages of the paper.

This arrangement prevailed for years, indeed decades. Suddenly it stopped. The paper arrived with its customary regularity but the written narrative was absent. Furthermore, there was no explanation forthcoming for its absence. Then again, neither gentleman phoned or wrote by what is now known as 'snail mail'.

Meantime, speculation abounded. Was Willie ill? Was Mary, the sister, ill? What could be amiss?

Then suddenly the old regime was re-established. There, in the margin, were Willie's observations. The Irish correspondent was back in business and all with his own literary style and panache.

"Dear Dan," he opened, "I would have written sooner but the pen was in the parlour."

An Adjustment of Views

It was away back in the immediate post-war period that I first heard of a wee, douce Scottish town, lying somewhere north of the Tay and south of the Don which was well-known – indeed almost infamous – for its distaste of Catholics and their religion.

It was not that the bulk of the folk were more zealous in their visible adherence to spirited Protestantism than was witnessed in the other small towns in that area. Kirk attendance was no worse and no better than that around them. It was just that they had a total distaste, distaste to the very borders of detestation, of everything Catholic.

Why it was so no-one seemed to know other than that it was so.

One consequence of this was that life was none too easy for the small Catholic population, of 300 or so, living in the town and the surrounding villages.

Then the small Catholic Church was given a new parish priest. Now it so happened that the garden of the parish house had an extensive garden which had a string of apple trees not too far from the garden wall.

By chance or by the intervention of the Holy Spirit the new parish priest had both green fingers and an expertise in apple trees. Of many a late morning or early evening he could be seen pruning or otherwise attending to his trees.

As the years slipped by folk going in and out of town could not help but notice his plentiful crop and notice him on his ladder. At first the changes were perfunctory, amounting to little more that a 'Good morning' or a 'Fine day' but out of such terse exchanges there grew sentences and, in due course, enquiries and requests for advice.

So it was the atmosphere changed. No-one converted to Rome but the cold air of evident hostility thawed somewhat with the result that with the further rolling of the years the wee town became well-nigh indistinguishable from those around it.

The change became more than discernible when residents on being introduced as being from that town and quizzed about their reputation for being far from keen on Papists, replied that both the townsfolk and the Roman Catholics were "nae different from ony ithers". Some even dropped the adjectival qualification.

The story of the town, the priest and the apple trees reminded me of my Aunt Nan.

My father was an only child so on his side of the family I had neither uncles nor aunts. My mother had been a Morrison of whom Nan was the youngest surviving child.

She had been born in 1900 and so was as old as the century. She served a seven-year apprenticeship as a dressmaker with a very fashionable, up-market shop in town (she was the only apprentice to live up a close).

In her early thirties she married a man from Sauchie, outside Alloa. After a brief honeymoon she found herself living in a house on the edge of Sauchie, her house being one in what is still known as a 'four in the block'.

Her front door looked out onto a large field: one year it would grow turnips or wheat, then it would be occupied by cattle, then it would produce cabbages, whereupon sheep would prevail. One year it lay fallow. It was all a very far cry from a tenement window looking into St Francis' Church in the Gorbals.

It appeared that her husband and his sister, who lived elsewhere in the village, had alerted the three other families in the block to the fact that the about-to-arrive bride was 'RC'.

We know nothing of their immediate reaction but I think we can take it that Nan was the first Catholic to come into their lives. I was very young at the time but I gleaned later that their immediate reaction was one of caution and apprehension, a situation exacerbated by the fact that she was from a big town, a city no less, and that her parents were both Irish.

Yet within months she had made herself acceptable and as the years rolled by she became a firm and trusted friend in all three of the households.

So what happened? Nan was neither ingratiating nor aloof. On the contrary, she was as she had always been, friendly and helpful yet without being intrusive.

Although from a working class family she had acquired some middle-class sophistication, partly from the fashion store in which she had worked and partly from the aspirants in her own family, not least her eldest sister who was in charge of an army of typists in the Invoice Department of a large wholesale store in Glasgow.

One result of this was that she subscribed to magazines and periodicals which were a shade or two more demanding than those read by the other three ladies in the block of four.

Having read her purchases she passed them on to the others. A not dissimilar situation arose about books. Nan was an avid reader and this activity was fortified by the demands of her husband's employment. He was in charge of the cocktail bar in the largest hotel in Alloa: as a result she was on her own for most of the evenings of the week.

So it was she recommended books and authors to her neighbours and frequently obtained the books for them from the local library.

This passing-on extended to recipes and patterns. It became a two-way street, the neighbours giving their advice on cooking certain dishes and giving advice on the merits or demerits of the shops in Alloa and the acceptability of local tradesmen and professionals.

Come the summer Nan would purchase material from a remnant shop in town and make summer dresses for the two wee schoolgirls in the Dunn family who lived above her.

Religion was almost never mentioned yet the neighbours could not help but notice that she travelled into Alloa every Sunday to attend Mass even when this involved, as it occasionally did, walking the four and a bit miles from Sauchie to the town.

Then again, when her son turned five she walked into town every school-day morning to put him into his Catholic school – and back again in the early afternoon to collect him.

So it was that Nan became acceptable, that a Catholic became acceptable. That did not make Catholicism acceptable but it did make Catholicism a shade less unacceptable and that was quite an achievement.

Shortly after the war ended Nan and her husband and son left Sauchie. The husband bought a public house near Glasgow Cross and they bought a house in Kings Park.

There were about 90 houses in the drive and as far as we knew Nan and her boy were the first Catholics. By all accounts, there she continued to practise the same basic kindness that she had always shown in Sauchie.

When her husband died the house was entrusted to her son and his family. She in turn moved to a modest flat in Crosshill.

On a murky, wet windswept night one February she was knocked down and killed in Cathcart Road. She was on her way to Vigil Mass.

This story first appeared in The Scottish Catholic Observer *of 3 February 2006. We are indebted to the Editor for her kind permission to include it in this collection.*

Political Distinction

My first attendance at the Salzburg Seminar in American Studies occurred in the late summer/early autumn of 1963.

The involvement was in no small measure attributable to my friend and colleague, Jim Livingstone.

Jim was a pathfinder to our group of part-time students at the Glasgow and West of Scotland Commercial College which, as it advanced, became the Scottish College of Commerce. We were all students pursuing degrees from the University of London and taking appropriate classes at this College which was located in Pitt Street in Glasgow, the building later becoming the Headquarters of Strathclyde Police.

Jim Livingstone was the first of our crowd to obtain his B.Sc. Econ., the first to take his M.Sc. and the first to be awarded his Ph.D. Others followed, but Jim was the pace-setter and navigator. His pioneering continued. He was the first of us to become a member of staff at the College and, appropriately, the first to be a Senior Lecturer. He was the first to have a textbook published and he was the first of us to attend the Salzburg Seminar, having seen an advertisement in *The Economist*. He had applied, been interviewed and accepted.

He was to be the first to have his own personal computer and not merely the first, but the only one of us to teach himself Chinese.

Having attended Salzburg in the very early sixties, he advised, encouraged and I suppose nagged me to follow in his footsteps, except that whereas he had attended a session on International Finance, he knew the rest of us would go for different topics and knew of my interest in American Politics and Government. It so happened that in 1962 I had taken an M.Sc. in Comparative

British and American Government, with a special emphasis on Political Parties.

When the Seminar published its programme for the academic year 1963-64 one session was on that same territory, so I applied, was interviewed and, like Jim, accepted.

In those days each session lasted four weeks. The tuition was by four or five specialists and there were usually some forty to sixty 'fellows' at the receiving end of the tuition.

We were advised or forewarned that the 'pitch' of the tuition would be at post-master level.

It will be seen, then, that the students or fellows were likely to be much of a muchness. This happy affinity was to be shattered in two quite opposite ways — and opposite —directions.

I had flown from Glasgow to London late on the Friday evening and on the Sunday about midday had reported to the Schloss where the Seminar was located. I was warmly welcomed by a Texas lady, the wife of the Director, a man called Harry Day.

I was the second fellow to arrive. I was introduced to the first arrival, a young man, a shade younger than myself. He was an Austrian from Vienna and his English was well-nigh perfect, spoken with an accent occasionally Viennese and occasionally American.

As we chatted and exchanged views on the current American scene, I was most interested by his detailed knowledge of the personnel of American politics: he knew the name of every Senator, not only his or her name and party and state, but also the names of those the incumbent had defeated first in the primary and then in the actual election. This was formidable but there was more, for he had similar detailed knowledge of most of the State Governors and more than fifty percent of the Members of the House of Representatives.

In a sense I was horrified. The University of London and I thought I was well-informed on that same scene, but this Austrian demonstrably knew much more that I did.

This eroded my confidence. It emerged, however, that he had poor to indifferent knowledge of American history. His knowledge was all of the present and the recent past, doubtless because he had spent twelve years in the States, the last eight years having been spent as a researcher in the headquarters of the Democratic Party. With this discovery my confidence rose.

Further re-assurance came through to me on the Monday and Tuesday. Both through work in class and chatter over meals in the magnificent dining room, it was soon evident that by far the majority of fellows were well-informed and most discussion could take place with a valid assumption as to prior knowledge. The Viennese gentleman proved to be an exception.

There was, too, another exception to the rule of acceptable prior knowledge. This exception centred on the group of seven Italians – six young men and one very attractive young lady, over whom the men were unduly and excessively protective. Later still, it was explained that Italian universities did not teach Politics. Most of the group had degrees in Law.

This lack of prior knowledge was to shock one of the tutors. At the end of a very well-delivered lecture on ethnic affiliation and party support, he invited questions. The first two came from a Londoner and a Swede. Both questions could be classified as bodyline bowling. Then the young Italian lady asked a question. Through indifferent English she observed that she knew that one of the two American parties was called the Democratic Party. What, she wanted to know, was the name of the other party?

At first the lecturer was not at all amused. Some of us thought that he thought she was 'having him on', but he managed to create a face, I suspect a façade, of benign avuncular and sympathetic understanding.

Thinking of those Salzburg Seminar days reminded me of a BBC programme of the early sixties. There was a General Election in the Republic of Ireland, and a young, able and conscientious reporter had been sent over by the BBC to the event. One evening, a day or two before the Election Day, his report on TV consisted of an interview with an elderly gentleman, a former Taoiseach. The interview took place in a garden by a grey pebble-dashed house in what looked like County Wicklow or Arklow. They were seated on an old wrought-iron bench. It was a good interview, indeed it was a very good interview. Clearly the young man knew his stuff and the elderly statesman was kind, considerate, thoughtful and quietly jovial – and wise. The interview reached a natural conclusion. The young man thanked the gentleman, maybe a shade too effusively, and brought the event to a close.

Then horror of horrors! We could 'see' an expression of panic cross the face of the young interviewer. One could sense and almost see the producer off-camera but gesticulating furiously at the young interviewer, telling him that he had misjudged the timing and that he, the producer, wanted two minutes more.

The young interviewer sighed audibly. Then, with a frog in his throat, he said: "Well, as I was saying, sir, that was a most informative and illuminating interview. We are very much in your debt but there is one matter we did not discuss and which I should have raised earlier. What exactly is the difference between Fianna and Fine Gail?"

A shudder of disapproval ran through the body of the statesman. His hitherto benign countenance now exhibited a sense of grave distaste, as though he had been asked a personal and penetrating question about his married life.

He shook his head sadly as though his earlier liking of, and his approval of, the interviewer had been mistaken.

"Well," he snorted, "I'll put it to you this way, young man. Those who have to know the difference know the difference and those who don't know the difference, don't need to know the difference." That said, he shook his head sadly and turned to look at the hills while the credits raced up the screen.

All the interviewer could be heard to say was: "Thank you, sir, thank you very much."

Professor Branton's Dilemma

It was said of Noel Branton that he knew everything yet knew no-one. Thus, if somebody asked who were on the Board of one of our leading companies, he could almost certainly name not only the Chairman, the Deputy Chairman and the Managing Director, but go on to identify almost all the Executive Directors and their areas of specialisation, and also name most of the non-executive Directors, providing a thumbnail sketch of each of them, including the other companies with which they were or had been identified.

Professor Noel Branton M.Com. Ph.D. was the first Dean of the School of Business and Administration in the University of Strathclyde. The first wave of Deans was appointed by the Senate at its inaugural meeting in the late summer of 1964. He was nominated by Alex Smith; I seconded the nomination. There were no further nominations for the Deanship and so that was that. Greatness was thrust upon him.

His involvement in the academic life of our conurbation dated from the late thirties. The Principal of a college in Cardiff, a man called Eric Thomson, was appointed Principal at the Glasgow and West of Scotland Commercial College with its then fairly modern building in Pitt Street. On assuming control of his new empire, the first thing Thomson did was to arrange that his Deputy in Cardiff should be suddenly and expeditiously translated to a similar post in Glasgow.

On Branton's arrival Thomson could relax: Branton would see and see competently to all the teaching which had to be undertaken. In addition, Branton would assess the market and recommend what further courses should be provided.

That was then. Come the middle sixties, a University environment constituted a very different situation.

The major difficulty here was that notwithstanding his knowledge, his own very successful teaching and his ability to recognise other competent and enthusiastic teachers, he was no social animal. He was married but there were no children and the couple had virtually no social life, apart, that is, from a very good and expensive holiday each summer. He had the air and demeanour of a quasi-recluse, a situation intensified by his myopic eye-glasses like the bottom of jam jars.

All that was in 1964 when the University was going through its birth pangs. Our story now moves forward to 1968 and 1969. By this time the establishment had settled and was progressing satisfactorily. In 1968 the Deans had completed their first spell in office. But now there was to be a difference. In keeping with John Eaton's vision of a modern, democratic University, Deans were to be elected, the electorate in each case to consist of the entire academic staff of the School or Faculty. Sadly, some Schools 'shirked the tackle' in football *patois* and simply reinstated the incumbent and in some cases did so by sycophantic acclamation. In the Business School, however, there was to be an election.

Notwithstanding his only too evident limitations, Branton was nominated. So too was another Professor, a man of somewhat eccentric and unpredictable behaviour. At a pre-Senate meeting of the Elected Members' Group one member asked whether it was true that the Business School was to have an election. (It was clear that he regarded this as extremely courageous.) On being told that it was true he asked what choice lay before the School's electorate. He was told that the choice lay between 'myopic inertia' and 'dynamic madness'. Myopic inertia was seen as the lesser of two evils. Noel Branton was re-elected.

During Prof Branton's first term in office a strange situation had arisen. Nothing was discussed, no formal decision was taken. Certainly nothing was recorded but I had acquired new and occasionally tricky yet demanding responsibilities. I had become a sort of sweeper-cum-advisor-cum-political commissar-cum-adjutant to the Dean. For his part, Branton never acknowledged all this, instead he simply availed himself of the situation as it had evolved.

One incident – as I recall it was in 1969 – illustrated this scenario.

One morning as I came out of a lecture theatre on the completion of an hour's teaching, I was confronted by his very capable secretary. "Oh, I'm so glad I caught you. He has a problem and wants to see you right away. Don't go for coffee. Just come with me and go in and see him."

When we reached the Dean's modest suite, I thanked the secretary, knocked on the door of his room and without waiting for an acknowledgement went in to see him. I told him that I understood he had a problem. I asked him what was amiss and what he wanted me to do, whereupon the story poured out of him.

It transpired that, although we had supposedly finalised our First Year intake for the new academic year, we were still receiving applications. One such was from a young man from a well-known West of Scotland family. The boy had more than our published minimum entry requirements; he just made our *de facto*, higher, real entrance level, though to be fair, he did make our standards. The only difficulty was that he was too late: we were full!

At this point I did not see the difficulty and said so. Yet the Dean writhed. The difficulty was that the Principal had telephoned and had urged the Dean to admit the youth.

I observed that was no difficulty. At that point my advice was succinct. "Comply," I advised.

That, however, did nothing to placate Branton. He pointed out that the Admissions Committee of Senate was already censuring the Schools which exceeded their allotted quotas. We were already one over quota. To go further incurred the risk of his being summoned before them to be rebuked.

"Okay," I said. "Reject him, and send a placatory note to the Principal, saying you would have been delighted to take the young man, but that we are over quota as it is, and as Chairman of the Senate, he — the Principal — will know that we are all expected to conform to Senate's pronouncements". But, note or no note, the answer was to reject the applicant.

The Dean was still far from happy. He observed that incurring the Principal's displeasure would be more dire than that of the Admissions Committee.

I observed that if he really believed the Principal's displeasure was the more serious of the two, then we were back to what I had originally advised: "Take him and be done with it," I declared.

Yet he wriggled and gave voice to his uncertainty. At this point I became a little too forceful. "All right," I said, "you do not want to attract the displeasure of the Principal or that of a key Senate Committee – so tell the Principal you are calling an Emergency Meeting of the Admissions Committee of the School and let them, the members, resolve the matter." Even as I said it, I knew this was the Pontius Pilate School of decision-making. But he grabbed it and the Admissions Committee, our own such committee, duly met in emergency session.

The meeting of the Committee started well enough but it soon degenerated into near chaos. The Dean, to his credit, gave a good, fair résumé of the situation and the dilemma which confronted us. We were between a rock and a hard place.

Whichever line we took we were fated to incur displeasure of either the Principal or the Senate Committee which might, for example, cut our quota for the entry of the following autumn. As for the Principal's ire, it could have a variety of unsavoury consequences. Which road did the members wish to travel?

Rather than answer, most of the members started asking questions, most of which were out of order or irrelevant. The Dean should have told them so but although he knew his Citrine as well as any of them he did not have the stern firmness to implement it. Instead, he tried to deal with the questions by providing a minimum of information. It was all rather reminiscent of a new batsman in with ten minutes to the tea interval!

"Why is the Principal so keen to have him aboard?"

"As already explained, he is a member of an important family."

"How important?"

"The Principal says very important."

"Does he have an 'A' level in Economics?" "Does he want to specialise in Accountancy?" "What school did he attend?"

The Dean chose to answer the school question.

"Gordonstoun," he observed.

Mary Dunn, our only female professor at that time, was sitting next to me.

"Do you know who it is?" she whispered to me.

I indicated that I did.

"Who is it?" persisted Mary.

"Charles," I said. Thereupon Mary gave voice to a semi-restrained shriek, swooned and fell to the floor.

Confusion ensued. Someone called for smelling salts. Two guys hauled her back to her chair. In the midst of this unbecoming situation Professor Branton showed uncharacteristic leadership. "I sense a small majority in favour of acceptance," he declared. "Does anyone demur?" he asked but by that time two members, a lady and a gentleman, started to take Mary Dunn back to her own room. The others collected their papers and the smelling salts and drifted away.

The young man was admitted. He had an indifferent First Year, a more successful Second Year, a markedly good Third Year. He went into an Honours Class and graduated with a highly commendable degree.

He was not called Charles.

And Professor Branton may that evening have shared a very small sherry with his wife.

Pollok 2209

"When the war is over and the fighting's done
and the boys come marching home............
A' the lassies will be kissing a' the laddies –
The laddies who fought and won".

The hostilities ended in 1945 and it was almost two years later, in 1947, before I was released from the RAF for which I had volunteered in 1942, before my eighteenth birthday.

When I arrived of an evening in Glasgow Central Station, complete with my pin-stripe navy 'demob' suit, not a single maiden or other young lady ran forward to embrace me and shower me with hot passionate kisses.

I was not surprised. I knew the song but I knew it was hyberbole. Nor was I resentful of the 'extra' two years service. Cynics (or the perceptive) said we had been retained because of the Cold War — in case it ceased being cold.

As I saw it, the Labour Government of Clement Atlee had been wise to let us out very gradually, like controlling very tightly the emission of air from a balloon. By adopting this policy of controlled release the Government went a long way towards ensuring that the jobs market was not inundated with hordes of work-seeking ex-servicemen and women.

In macro-economic terms one of the Government's policies was that of full employment, which allowing for the movement of and within the labour market meant that unemployment should not exceed 3% and in that aim the Government was most successful.

The house to which I returned was familiar: it was a three-apartment Council or Corporation house in Govanhill which we had been allocated in 1934.

The difference was that my father had died in 1942 between my volunteering and being summoned for aircrew training. My grandmother had died in 1944 while I was in South Africa.

The household consisted of my mother, then in her middle fifties, and me.

My mother had succeeded in obtaining a congenial, albeit not very well paid, job as a sort of non-qualified nurse in a very large primary school. For my part my new Civil Service post paid a reasonable if not yet handsome salary with the further attraction of annual increments.

It was not riches beyond the dreams of avarice but it was a start on a long march to middle-class prosperity – and social status.

That said, we were barely out and running when we went down a rather ugly snake in the snakes and ladders board of life.

What happened was that having been based at Kinning Park Employment Exchange for the four months of my induction period, I was posted to Troon.

A family discussion resolved that I should not go and live in digs in Troon. My mother had no wish to go back to living on her own.

Travelling daily, however, was going to be expensive as well as necessitating an early start to the working day and an erosion of one's evenings. On the first of these matters my two maiden aunts were generosity itself in offering to pay for some of my travelling.

The record books of the Department would show I spent eight months at Troon Employment Exchange, but for two months of that spell I was at home, suffering from rheumatic fever contracted when I was soaked in a thunderstorm one day in Troon, when I had gone out on a call without a raincoat. I had to work the rest of the day and then travel home in the wet clothing.

Yet I keep observing that the Holy Spirit works in strange ways.

My medical condition merited a transfer back to Glasgow and a shorter, markedly shorter, travel. I was allocated to Bridgeton Exchange where I met my wife and where I encountered Miss Lamb who was, as I saw it, substantially responsible for my premature promotion in 1954.

More, being in Glasgow allowed me to attend classes in the evenings and that in turn, over the ensuing eight years, led to a one-year Certificate in Unemployment Benefit, the three-year Diploma in Public Administration of the University of Glasgow and the four-year course leading to Honours in the renowned B.Sc. Economics of the University of London.

In short, the rheumatic fever did not do my heart any good but the rest of me was the beneficiary.

As I recall it, it was sometime in 1949 or 1950 that my mother and I decided we should aspire to having a telephone installed. We were given the number – Pollok 2209.

It then transpired that the number for Third Lanark Football Club and their park or stadium was Pollok 0029. This soon gave rise to disconcerting inconvenience.

In August and September it was not too bad but in those days prior to flood-lighting the kick-off in December and January moved back into the very early afternoon.

So it was the phone would ring, and a voice asked: "When's the kick-off?" or "When does ra match start?"

Then the fixture list would become involved. The phone would ring. "Is that Cathkin? Who are we playing ra day? Is it Falkirk? An' when's the kick-aff?"

All of this occurred on a Saturday so, since I was working, my mother had to deal with it as best she could. She strove to explain that the caller was not on to Cathkin but it was almost always to no avail.

"Ur you ra wee wummin that makes ra tea? Go and get us somebody that knows about the fitba'."

As the weeks went by the queries would extend to team selection.

"Is McLeod playing? If he's no' playing, then we're no' coming, so we're no'!"

We tried to have our number changed but to no avail. Moreover, I lacked the courage and audacity of the business man in Hope Street, who found to his intense chagrin that his phone number was very like that of the Booking Office of the Alhambra Theatre. Prior to, and during the Pantomime Season and in summer during the months of the 'Five Past Eight' Show, his phone was continually ringing with enquiries as to price and the availability of seats. Like me, he tried to have his number changed. Like me, he failed.

Eventually he wrote to the phone authorities and to the manager of the Alhambra saying that unless his phone number was altered by a certain date he would direct his staff to purport to accept bookings and to tell callers to "just collect your tickets and pay for them on the night". I was told that the first night the callers complied, that is, went to the box office with banknotes at the ready, all chaos prevailed:

"But I was told.....".   "I was given an assurance......."

Well-dressed ladies were sniffling or crying, weans were bawling, men were irate. Normal customers – with their tickets at the ready – could barely get through the foyer.

It was dreadful yet it had the desired result. Before a week was out the business man had a new number. It was not unlike that of a firm selling church organs, so there was no great disturbance.

For our part we succumbed. Of a Saturday before I left about ten past eight, I would give my mother a cup of tea in her bed and a slip of paper and go over it with her. "As you see here, they are playing Ayr United. The game is due to start at 2 o'clock and there is the team selection."

As the months and years went by we prospered but Third Lanark unfortunately went into decline and eventually disappeared.

The late Robert Crampsey used to relate a tale of their declining years.

By the time of this story they were in the Second Division. While they had been a First Division outfit they had been obliged to have a new ball for each home game, whereas, in the Second Division this new ball provision applied to every second, and every alternative home game.

All that said, there were strong rumours they were not complying with the provision. For example, it was said that occasionally they would varnish an old ball so that, viewed from the stand, it looked like a new ball.

At the end of one game the manager was approached by a referee, who, being 'idle' that Saturday, had attended their game. He explained that not only would he be 'doing' their next home game but the inspector of referees would be in the stand to review his performance. He went on to argue that it was essential that they got everything right. "For example," he went on to say, "you really must have a new ball. Now don't let me down. Don't let yourselves down."

The poor manager was in a tiz. He knew how tight the financial position was. Nevertheless he telephoned the Chairman and begged for the money to buy a new ball.

But the Chairman was for none of it. His niece, he claimed, would see to it. "The young lady has contacts," he explained. "You have my assurance," he told him. "There will be a new ball on your desk by noon on the day of the game."

On the day of the match the manager arrived at two minutes beyond noon. He raced into his room and, as promised, there was a brand new ball sitting in all its glory in the middle of his desk. Even so the manager screamed!

He lifted it and examined it and determined what he had suspected. The new ball was a size 4, as used in some sections of school football and not a size 5 used throughout the senior game.

Later he learned the young lady had seen the ball at a 'sale' price in Lumley's window. She had seen it from the upper deck of a No 3 tram on her way home from University to Pollokshields. Responding to her sense of duty, she alighted at the next stop and hastened back to Lumley's to make the purchase.

A new dilemma confronted the manager. As soon as the referee reported, he accosted him and between them they conjured up a solution.

This ploy involved the manager inflating the ball until the sphere although not a size 5 was about 4.4 or 4.5. He, the referee, would take it out and place it on the centre spot. The manager was to tell his players that as early as possible – in the first minute if possible – a forward should pass the ball all the way back to one of the full-backs or the centre-half.

Whoever received it was to kick it to the goalkeeper who had to be told to appear to squeeze it and look askance at it and gesticulate to the referee, who being a party to the conspiracy, would be ready to run all the way to the keeper. He would take the ball, examine it, and in turn gesticulate to the pavilion. Thereupon he would divest himself of the new ball and some old turnip of a ball would be thrown to him, whereupon he would give it to the goalkeeper who would kick it out.

The world and the SFA would be satisfied. They would have started the game with a new ball.

But Burns said it all:

"*The best laid schemes of mice and men*
   Gang aft agley
And leave us nought but grief and pain
   For promised joy".

The inside-right did his job to perfection. When he got the ball instead of punting it out to the winger he kicked it all the way back to his centre-half. His reward was a torrent of abuse for his inexplicable play.

Unfortunately the centre-half was not the brightest of men. Moreover, years of heading heavy wet balls had not improved his I.Q. Instead of passing the ball back to the goalkeeper, as instructed, he enthusiastically thumped it up the park.

His counterpart in the visiting team was getting ready to head it, but as the ball flew through the air, it visibly diminished in size and looked like a miniature flying saucer. As it completed its flight it was seen to be concave and settled like a 'bunnet' on the head of the visiting centre-half.

The air was out of the ball and the air was clearly out of Third Lanark.

It was a much admired and beloved club. Like Clyde, which still staggers on, it had its own particular and peculiar support, the characteristics of which were patience, resilience, hope – and resignation to hostile Fate.

Mr Cuthbertson

The brash, the rude and the thoughtless referred to him as 'Cubbie'. Significantly, however, the rest of us, not least those who were senior to him, invariably addressed him as 'Mr Cuthbertson'. This included a very clever, very efficient but somewhat haughty Higher Executive Officer who was about to become a Senior Executive Officer. He addressed some, indeed most, juniors and equals by their stark surname. "Smithers, are the statistics available yet? Well, get on with it, man!" He also addressed 'Cubbie' as 'Mr Cuthbertson'.

Mr Christopher Cuthbertson was one of the most gentle and one of the finest men I ever encountered. He was about sixty years of age and was Senior Clerical Officer in an outpost of our Scottish HQ in Edinburgh. We were located in a mid-terrace villa in a cul-de-sac running alongside the southern wall of the Episcopal Seminary.

He shared a desk with another Edinburgh man – a good sort but without the magnetic appeal of Mr Cuthbertson. They sat opposite each other on opposing sides of their large desk which was located in the top floor bay window.

I did not know Mr Cuthbertson for long. The staffing level of this section warranted 2.5 Junior Executive Officers. At the time I was located in a similar but larger unit, in Glasgow. The 0.5 was made up by my being sent there on 3 days and then 2 days in alternate weeks.

Mr Cuthbertson's line of command did not go through me or any of the other two Junior Executives. Instead he answered directly to the Higher Executive Officer.

He was very much a private person but opened up a bit at lunch-time when he ate his sandwiches and made himself a mug of tea.

We developed a restrained rapport. I learned that he was a widower, was an elder in a church off the main road from Tollcross to Morningside and that he lived with his married daughter, her husband and their seven-year-old son.

What moved us a notch or two closer occurred when it transpired one day that he and his family had spent that year's summer holiday at Fairhaven on the east coast of the Cumbrae, one of the islands in the Firth of Clyde. I won a few brownie points when I told him that I knew Fairhaven well.

Mr Cuthbertson's accommodation that year was a substantial house of yellow sandstone, now weathered to a cream. From time to time it had been a private residence but Mr Cuthbertson and his family caught it when it was a hotel.

He and his grandson loved it. Each morning after breakfast the young couple would leave to walk into Millport, always bringing back newspapers, an occasional comic, sweets and chocolate.

While they were away, Mr Cuthbertson would sit on the rocks and read the preceding day's papers while his grandson pottered about on the pockets of sand or played with a small wooden boat in the pools. Occasionally the boy would paddle and delighted in jumping out of the way of the modest waves made by the many turbines and paddle steamers as they sailed though the Largs channel.

In the afternoons he might go for a nap or if the weather was indifferent he would play with the boy.

After their high tea all four would go for a gentle walk along one of the three roads that radiated out of Fairhaven.

"You know," he said one day, "I have never had a better holiday. But I would not repeat it lest it blunted my wonderful memories."

Such then was our Mr Cuthbertson: conscientious, loyal, oozing common sense and innately decent. As I see it, the Mr Cuthbertsons are the backbone of the nation. In their quiet diligent ways they are an example for the rest of us, not least for the greedy, the selfish and the brutally ambitious.

My ten weeks passed all too quickly. Sadly I never saw Mr Cuthbertson again.

Huey Long

Mrs McKendrick never knew about Huey Long. He was far beyond her field of interests. On the other hand, if she had known about him, her profound assessment of him would have been that he was 'not a nice man'.

Mrs McKendrick would have been correct. For Huey Long was a bit of a scoundrel: he was an American politician who was one of those who brought politics and politicians into disrepute. When he was murdered, assassinated on the steps of his State Legislature, few Americans mourned: while deploring the cause of his departure, most of them thought the U.S.A. was a cleaner country now that he had gone.

One story – oft repeated – tells us much about him.

The story has it that one day while electioneering he looked out over and at his not inconsiderable audience and proclaimed:

"There is one other matter I would raise. It is this. I would have you know that I envy many of you good people. Why? Because many of you have been given the great gift of faith. I wasn't: that wonderful gift somehow passed me by. But I know what it is to have that wonderful gift. I know because I knew two ladies who had it in abundance.

"You see, when I was a boy of 15 or so, I used to rise early of a Sunday morning. I used to hitch my horse to my cart and then go over to my Catholic grandmother's house and take her to her early Sunday morning mass. I would sit outside reading the sports pages of the Sunday papers. Then when she and the other folks came out, I would take her home and she would give me the finest breakfast a boy could have. When we were finished we would wash the dishes and I would leave and go over to the house of my

Methodist grandmother and take her to the 11 o'clock service in her Methodist church. Again I would sit outside, but there was no reading of Sunday papers for that hour and a half. Again when the service ended and these good Christian folks would emerge I would take her home and in no time at all she would conjure up a delicious lunch that delighted my taste buds. In her house I didn't help with the dishes for she had a coloured girl, a maid of sorts, who saw to all that. Instead she would take me to the door and slip a coin or two to me before kissing me and seeing me off.

"So there it is. That is how I got to know about the gift of faith.

"I remember those wonderful ladies and I hope that come Election Day you will remember me and vote for me. May your God bless you all."

Later, back in their hotel, Huey and his coterie were helping themselves to a liberal supply of strong drink.

"Huey," cried one rogue, "I never knew you had a Methodist grandmother."

"And another thing," cried a colleague, "I certainly didn't know you had a Catholic grandmother."

"Hell," said Huey by way of reply, "I didn't even have a horse."

Louis Bean

As I recall it, Louis Bean was a small, neat, dapper sort of man, invariably 'well-turned out'. Yet, that said, he was not to the fore in any gathering. It was hard to be sure why this was the case. True, his lack of inches was something of a hindrance on such occasions. Then again, although his clothing was of good quality and could be said to suit him, he tended to go for dull, drab colours. Finally his manner tended to be severe or – a possible reservation - was construed as being off-putting.

Louis Bean had trained with a view to becoming a mathematician. As his career developed his interest in politics intensified and so it was he married the two disciplines and transformed himself into a psephologist – someone who studies election statistics and the patterns of how people vote. Louis became not only a good, a competent psephologist, but an outstandingly successful psephologist.

What Louis Bean had discerned and the others had missed was that many of the farmers in the Mid-West had come to like the subsidies they had received during the war years, subsidies which Truman had retained and was promising to continue with. Normally the Republican-voting farmers opposed subsidies and favoured minimum government. What had happened was that enlightened self-interest had caused the see-saw tilt. The farmers remained sceptical about subsidies in general but they liked the subsidies which they received and wanted to go on receiving them.

This was to prove important.

When I met Louis Bean at the Salzburg seminar I had the benefit of attending his lectures and tutorials and of chatting with him over meals and, on occasion, over a drink of an evening.

With that in mind I can say that the essence, the back-bone of his theory, was that an individual vote is determined by three factors – your brain, your heart and your wallet. This does not call for much elaboration but it required some. By brain, he had in mind your intelligence and reasoning ability. This facility should enable you to discern, to identify weak fallacious arguments and so to disregard them and those who endeavour to advocate them. By the same token valid reasoning is to be acknowledged.

The wallet factor is again almost self-explanatory. Would you be a beneficiary of certain policies? Alternatively: would they cost you and diminish rather than increase your spending power?

All that said, it could be that an individual could look favourably on a policy which involves higher taxation but takes the view that the policy is so attractive and worthy of implementation that the higher tax is, in this instance, of no great import.

The heart is a somewhat trickier factor in that it has two quite different connotations. Firstly, it can be a factor of charity, of compassion – such as helping the poor. It can also have the different factor of blood. Is a candidate a member of your tribe? This is a big factor in many African-based communities. Or, again, in quasi-tribal societies such as Northern Ireland.

In its simpler form Bean's theory was this:

• If all three factors point the one way, then the electoral option of such folk is absolutely clear. Such individuals tend to be somewhat intolerant.

• The happy and contented individuals are those for whom two factors point decisively one way and the residual factor goes the other way. These individuals tend to be the bed-rock of a political party's support.

• The third element consists of those who have two factors pulling them in totally opposite directions while the residual factor keeps bobbing one way and then the other. Such folk are the natural 'don't knows' of the pre-election polls. It is a slightly worrying, disconcerting thought that these ditherers cause the political pendulum to swing and so determine the outcome of the elections.

So there it is. Louis Bean's theory is attractively simple.

Yet I knew a professor of Political Theory in a large middle-west University in the States who argued that Louis was not always as clear as he might have been on the subject of what political weighting he gave to his three factors.

The mid-west man told me he gave the brain and the wallet 30% each, but that he gave the heart 40% — which enabled him to give 20% to each of our two concepts of the heart – the dimension of compassion and the tribal.

The ultimate proof of Louis Bean's theory came when he was the only commentator to say that Truman would beat Dewey in the American Presidential election of 1948.

In the weeks prior to the election his was a lone voice, so much so that some other commentators scoffed at him. Mrs Dewey, the wife of the Republican candidate, was so confident her husband would win she ordered new curtains for the White House.

The Lovely Blue Dress

The heroine of this story is a Glasgow lady now in her early eighties and living in her well-run, very presentable home on the south-side of the city.

When she was a teen-age schoolgirl in the war and the immediately post-war years, she did extremely well and so it came as no surprise to her teachers and fellow pupils when she left in 1947 with a very healthy clutch of Scottish Highers, all at impressive grades.

Normally a girl of that diligence, intelligence and aptitude would have progressed, 'gone up' to the University of Glasgow at Gilmorehill, but the family circumstances deemed otherwise. Her father, a small, hard-working man, was on a modest salary and worked long and hard hours including two nights each week behind the bar of a busy city pub. The heart of the matter was that the household was deemed to need a further wage each week and rightly or wrongly the parents reckoned they had done well to let her stay at school as long as she had.

So it was she sat the Clerical Officers' Examination of the Civil Service Commissioners, an exam she passed with ease with the result that within weeks she was advised of her success, assigned to the Ministry of Labour and told to report to the Employment Exchange in Rutherglen, just outside the city's boundaries. She was to serve there, in three offices in Glasgow and as far east as Coatbridge and as far west as Dunoon in Argyll.

Our story now moves forward to the late sixties of the last century. By this time our heroine has married and lives with her husband and her three children in a pleasant house in King's Park. Moreover, she has re-trained as a teacher and is teaching in a school in East Renfrewshire. Her husband teaches in town and is active in the three wings of the Labour Movement. As though that were not enough, his activities extend to the Fabian Society. This year, he tells her, there is to be a special Fabian dinner in town. There are to be two speakers, a Cabinet Minister up from London while he, her beloved husband, is to be the support speaker.

It is this news which leads to her resolving to make a dress, a long evening dress, equal to the occasion, whereupon she obtains a pattern and then buys a length of a magnificent velvet material of a delightful shade of blue. For weeks thereafter she is working on what becomes known as 'the lovely blue dress' and of course all this activity is in addition to teaching at school, marking homework, shopping, cooking and washing and ironing at home and attending to the three children to say nothing of a husband who as often as not is out of an evening at yet another meeting. Miraculously it all went well and the lovely blue dress was ready.

The evening of the dinner started well. The Minister was infamous for running late, but remarkably he was punctual – indeed he was a few minutes early. Better still: he was extremely sociable. He mixed with the members and their guests, he signed autographs and posed for photographs.

One result was that this dinner started on time. The waitresses were both efficient and fleet of foot and it was clear that the speech would start on time.

During the meal the chat went well while the food was most acceptable.

The dessert was apple pie and cream. The waitresses served the apple pie and put large jugs of cream on each table. The top table warranted three such jugs, one towards each end and a particularly large jug in the middle.

The Chairman started worrying, unnecessarily, about his timetable and foolishly announced a comfort break while the coffee was being served, thus causing confusion at some tables.

The lady's husband due to be the first speaker rose, stretched himself and in doing so extended his arm, knocked over the largest jug of cream from which the cream spewed out over the tablecloth and onto the blue, the hitherto lovely blue velvet dress.

In an instant the wearer of the dress knew that her night was ruined. So too was her dress, the output of her hours of labour and —unless she was charitable in the extreme — her marriage.

People shrieked and cried, napkins were proffered and the ill-informed talked of dry cleaners, but she knew it was all useless – totally of no avail.

The Chairman returned from his comfort break, tasted his cold coffee, called the guests to order and gave his brief, succinct opening remarks and called on his first speaker to give his address.

This the husband did. As he spoke, there was occasional desultory applause, but many of those present were looking at one another sharing perplexity. His material was good but there was no panache, no style, no expertise in timing or emphasis.

When he finished his speech the minimal applause did not last long.

Fortunately the Minister, a polished performer, was at his best. He provided laughter, winning cries of support and agreement, touching on delight. When he finished he was given a standing ovation.

While all this was going on our heroine was sitting in misery and remorse while the milky fluid seeped through her dress, through her under-garments and onto her skin.

When the night was over they left sharply and then drove home in an ominous silence. When they were home in the house she grabbed a dressing gown and disappeared into the bathroom.

No one ever saw the dress again. No-one spoke of it, no-one mentioned it then. No-one does now.

The heroine was and is my wife Ellen. I was and am the clumsy oaf of a husband. I always was and am awkward and clumsy. Should you want – although why should you want – beetroot or whisky spilled, I am your man.

Remarkably, perhaps with the grace of God, we are still married.

Eegeewapetee

Elsewhere in these stories I have told of my aunt Nan, the youngest of the Morrison family, marrying a man from Sauchie, outside Alloa in Clackmannanshire. She lived on the very edge of the village. She spent a lot of each day on her own because her husband was in charge of the cocktail bar in the Crown Hotel, the leading hotel, indeed the only hotel of note, in Alloa.

Of a day, they would rise late. They would have breakfast which was very late by Sauchie standards and he would leave by nine-thirty to catch his bus into town. Like many others in the licensing trade then, he was off duty for three hours, from 2pm till 5pm, of an afternoon and then resume his duties from 5 until 10pm. He would come home for about 2.30pm for a lunch-cum-dinner and a short sleep and leave about 4.20pm for the bus back into town. His working day ended with his coming home shortly after 10.30pm when they would have a light supper and go to bed as midnight approached. They did not have much time for bright conversation.

One day in the first year of the marriage the husband arrived in about 2.40. As he divested himself of his coat, he remarked that he was a shade later as he had been speaking to "Eegeewapetee". Nan had heard about the lady who lived in a cottage on the main street of the village. She was a village worthy. Now in her middle eighties she was not merely heavy but gross. As a result she was not very mobile. In good weather, however, she would sit outside her cottage and hold court with all who came her way.

Though she did not get out and about, she was remarkably well informed on the affairs of state of Sauchie. She was moderately interested in Alloa but there her curiosity and her quest for news terminated.

But why was she known as Eegeewapetee? For the answer to that question we have to go back to the middle years of the nineteenth century and to the middle years of the reign of Victoria.

One day a girl of about 10, a clever girl and a precocious girl, was in the one-class village school. The teacher was taking the older children for spelling. She was working from a book and was concentrating on the names of countries. England and Wales, Scotland and Ireland were quickly discussed and so she rushed off into Europe. France, Spain, Italy and Greece did not give rise to much difficulty.

The same was true of the Scandinavian nations. Then the teacher turned to Africa. So it was she looked at our girl. "Spell Egypt," she instructed, and the girl bounced to her feet, omitted the 'Please, miss' and almost shouted "Eegeewapetee".

Moreover, she did not speak – or roar – slowly. On the contrary, she almost spat it out. The teacher gaped at her. Then thinking the teacher did not understand it she repeated it and was even louder and faster.

From that moment onwards she was known to her peer group as "Eegeewapetee".

When she died it was said that folk, including some from Fishcross and Alva, attended the burial just to hear her real name in the mouth of the minister. This is how they learned about her. Yet within a twelve-month no-one could recall her full proper name. In talking about her, in referring to her they spoke always of "Eegeewapetee".

Fundamentals

This incident occurred in the early sixties - in the year or two before the Scottish College of Commerce was merged with or, depending on your point of view, was taken over by the Royal College of Science and Technology to become the University of Strathclyde.

The Principal of the Scottish College was a Dr Eric Thomson. He had done a good job, a very good job in transforming the gey wobbly Glasgow and West of Scotland Commercial College into a highly successful tertiary College with a high percentage of its students obtaining external degrees from the University of London.

In one of the Honours Lists he was awarded a C.B.E. At the time most of the staff saw this as a reward for a job well done. A perceptive few saw it as a consolation prize. Left on its own, the continuing success of the Scottish College might just have earned Thomson a knighthood. That would not occur in Strathclyde where the Royal College of Science and Technology Principal, Dr Samuel C. Curran, who became the University Principal, would be given a knighthood.

As it was, the glee of the majority of the Scottish College staff prevailed and a celebratory dinner was happily arranged. This dinner was hold in More's Hotel in India Street.

Staff members had to buy tickets for the event and the price included a surcharge for the presentation to Dr Thomson 'to mark the occasion'. On the night in question there was, of course, a top table. So far as the body of the kirk was concerned there was a table plan but no cognizance had been taken of status or discipline. It was then a matter of pot luck (or bad luck) who was beside you or opposite you.

I cannot remember who was across the table from me. What I remember was that on my right side was Sheena McKinlay, a bright breezy lady who, like me, was an external B.Sc.Econ. from London. On my left I had a man called Fuller who was Director of the Scottish Hotel School which was a sub-set of the Scottish College and whose School was in Ross Hall out at Crookston. The building is now a private hospital. Fuller's other claim to fame was that his brother was Professor of Poetry at Oxford.

In due course the ladies came round with the food. When it came to the main course, the leading lady put two pieces of meat on each plate. She was followed by the gravy lady who in turn was followed by the potato lady, then the carrot and cucumber lady.

As the leading lady put the two pieces of meat on his plate, Fuller waved his menu and touched the lady's fore-arm. "I know what it purports to be," he declared, "but what in fact is it?" he asked.

"Ach, what the hell does it matter?" answered the lady. "Efter a'," she declared, "it a' works oot the same; it a' works oot as ....." and here she refrained from using a noun, proper or improper, gave him a knowing nudge and proceeded on her way. Fuller was silenced, which was an unusual state of affairs.

The Mystery of the Lady in the Passenger Seat

The origins of the story lie in an academic year in the closing stages of the seventies.

In our University we were fortunate to have an outstanding Professor of Politics; indeed, he was of international renown. His research portfolio was most impressive and his books sold well throughout the English-speaking world and had been translated into diverse other languages. So successful were his books that it was said he at least trebled or quadrupled his University salary by the royalties which followed his writing. Nor was that all. He was a psephologist with the result that at times of elections and those of political crisis he seemed to live either in TV and radio studios or in the taxis hustling him from one broadcasting institution to another.

Judged by such success he was seen as a treasure and others in other political departments said we were lucky to have him. Yet he could be difficult and there were those who found him, on occasions, to be almost incoherent.

On one famous occasion he invited me to move to his department and be a sort of adjutant while he did his commanding officer. I declined. More, although I thanked him, I pointed out that were I to accept we would almost certainly find ourselves living in ongoing civil war.

All this being as it was I was more than a little surprised when, one day in late October, he telephoned me. I have had short succinct phone calls and I have had long rambling calls. This one was towards the latter end of the curve.

Nevertheless, I followed the drift of it.

He had with him a young Jewish post-graduate student. The student, Israel Peleg, had arrived in Glasgow from the Hebrew

University in Jerusalem. He had travelled to the city to sit at the feet of the great man. He had done so as he was working for a Ph.D. on the Impact of Broadcasting on Politics. It should have been a dream academic situation – an enthusiastic student and an academic who was a leading authority on the researcher's subject. It should have gone well: on the contrary it had gone badly, very badly.

The second half of the call was a request. He had pointed out that there was a man in another department who had a degree in Politics and who had an involvement in broadcasting. At the time I was the Scottish member on the Independent Broadcasting Authority and had been doing the job since January 1970. The question at issue was: would I be prepared to see Mr Peleg and go on seeing him? In short: would I take him for the rest of the academic year?

I said I would – and within five minutes, my secretary was bringing the young man into my room.

It went wonderfully well.

He and I responded well to each other and I was able to arrange for him to see managing directors and programme controllers of both Television and Radio companies and, in some instances, the equivalent BBC executives. These interviewing possibilities extended to the political commentators employed by the broadcasters and the political party officials and elected representatives.

I know we were both sorry to see our 'year' end and he returned to round off his studies in Israel.

In due course I was delighted – but not surprised – when he was awarded his Doctorate.

A few years later there was a General Election in Israel. It was won by the Labour Party. I knew Dr Peleg was friendly with Peres, the Labour Party leader who was the new Prime Minister.

I bought *The Times* to see if I could spot some reference to Israel Peleg but did not find anything of that nature.

Some six months or so thereafter, however, I received a letter from the Israeli Embassy in London.

Written on expensive, impressive, notepaper it told me that a party of senior British journalists was being invited for a ten-day tour of Israel, travelling as guests of the Israeli Government. It went on to say that Dr Israel Peleg, the Director of Information Services for the Israeli Government, was insisting that my name be added to the list.

Six or eight weeks later I found myself at the EL AL desk at Heathrow and was delighted to find my colleagues on the trip included the late Hugh Cochrane of the Glasgow *Evening Times*. We were all impressed by the security control exercised by the EL AL staff and, special guests or not, they made sure of our acceptability before entrusting us with boarding passes.

Being poor at languages, I like, when I travel, to know there is someone in the country of destination who knows me and could testify and/or take action on my behalf.

In this instance I was fortunate in that through the Salzburg Seminar on American Studies, I knew Judge Shoshana Berman of the High Court of the Israeli Judiciary, to whom I wrote telling her of my impending visit.

While I was there I managed to see Israel Peleg on three occasions. In particular I remember sitting with him and his wife in an open-air café in Tel Aviv as midnight approached. There were about 300 customers and everyone, except me, seemed to be talking.

I also received a phone call from Shoshanna who let me know she was holding a buffet supper that night in her home at Richovat. She graciously suggested I join her and her guests.

I was for it, but how was I to get there?

"By taxi," suggested Shoshana.

I demurred. I reminded her I was a Scot. "We are not mean – but we are prudent. I have no intention of paying half the Israeli National Debt."

Shoshana took the point and said she would ring back.

Eventually she did. She said Dr Otto Schlesinger, the Israel Director of the Ford Foundation, was willing to uplift me provided, first, he would not actually stop his car: he would bring it down to about 5 miles per hour, whereupon I could jump in, the door being ready to be opened. A second provision was that I should tell them how I would be dressed. I agreed.

It worked. Precisely on time his large Ford rolled into the forecourt. He indicated his back door. I opened it and tumbled onto the back seat.

Introductions were mumbled so I did not catch the name of the lady in the passenger seat.

The journey, most of it through the dark of the Israeli countryside, took about an hour. Occasionally I was brought into the conversation but most of the conversation was confined to Schlesinger and the lady. Sometimes they spoke English but in other instances it was in German or Yiddish.

But who, what, was she? At the time I thought it was his wife but occasional intonations made me think they were not married – or at least, not to each other. Was she a girl friend – or his mistress? Here, at times, both intonation and body language suggested there was something of that nature. Yet within minutes I was abandoning such conclusions.

So it was the mystery continued.

Such, then, was the first aspect of the mystery. It was a matter of relationship.

As it is put in the concluding line of the well-known, slightly rude limerick: "Who's who, what's what and who's doing what to whom?"

The second aspect of the mystery was of origins. What nationality was she? Was she an Israeli? Had she been German? Was she now an American citizen?

As we trundled through the dark, speculation scurried along. One moment I thought I had the answers. Within five minutes I had abandoned it in favour of a totally different 'solution'.

When we reached Shoshana's home some twenty or so guests were already there. Within an hour this had doubled. Protracted conversation was not easy, particularly after the food was available.

Nevertheless it was like working on a large jigsaw. Slowly yet surely the picture was emerging.

By the time of departure I had most of my answers: in part confirmed by the further intelligence that the lady was not returning to Tel Aviv. On the contrary, she was staying overnight in Shoshana's house.

As I sat in the passenger seat of the Ford and as Schlesinger drove I mulled over the story as I understood it.

The lady and Shoshanna were life-long friends. Their childhood had been spent in a small town outside Kiev in the then Soviet Union. They had gone to school together and had sat next to each another.

Then the Germans violated the treaty they had with the Soviet Government. They invaded and the citizens of the Soviet Union found they were at war.

Some two or three months after their war began, a local Communist Party dignitary and a minor executive from Moscow arrived and announced that some – most – of the Jewish community was seen as 'unreliable' and was to be 're-located' in the east, some 250–300 kilometres beyond the Urals.

The transportation resulted in the girls being separated. They and their respective families were in different villages about 100 kilometres apart.

Yet the separation was not total. Shoshana had a lively, dynamic aunt who worked in a former tractor factory which, by then, was making tanks. She had a one-week holiday each year. This was spent hitch-hiking to the village where their separated friends and neighbours were resident. She took small presents and lots of news – who had died, who was born, who was working where. On her return she had not dissimilar news to impart and small gifts to distribute.

Then in May 1945 when the Red Army was at the doors of Berlin men arrived in their villages and announced they were from the Jewish 'underground' force and that it had been decided - they did not reveal by whom - to get out them of the USSR.

They would return in a week to collect the children and, again, a few weeks later to uplift the adults.

"Where are we going?" the adults asked.

"The west," declared the visitors.

"Near Kiev?" suggested an adult.

"Further," was the succinct reply.

In the wake of their transportation the girls – now teenagers – found themselves re-united in an old army barracks in Poland.

They had been assigned to a 'school' and again they were sitting next to each another.

Four weeks after their arrival in the barracks, both sets of parents joined them.

But before 1945 was out, the two men from the 'underground' re-appeared.

"This isn't going to work," they announced.

"This country is going to go Communist as well," they contended. "Get the children ready and again we'll return for the adults."

As a result of their second movement, the girls found themselves in the French Zone of Germany. Again they were in school and again they were sitting next to each other.

This time the parents of the mystery lady arrived fairly promptly but as 1945 rolled over and 1946 evolved, Shoshana's parents had not arrived and consequently were deemed to be 'missing'.

Then one night at the depth of the night, Shoshana was awakened by the redoubtable aunt.

"Shoshana," she proclaimed, "I have found your parents. I will have them here within a week. Now go back to sleep. Goodnight." — as though any sensitive child could return to sleep in such circumstances.

Within a week, Shoshana and her parents were re-united.

Some six months later the same two Jewish 'underground' gentlemen reappeared. Their announcement had a distinct *déjà vu* quality.

"This isn't going to work," they announced.

"It is a case of 'next year in Jerusalem'," they proclaimed.

"We're going to take you to Israel," they declared, and continued, "there will be no separation. We will take you as families."

And they were as good as their word. They did 'smuggle' both families into what we now see as Israel.

Within a year both families were in Jerusalem and our two girls, now young women, were students at the Hebrew University in Jerusalem. This time they were separated as Shoshanna studied Law while her friend did Modern Languages.

In due course Shoshana married an artist while her friend married an architect.

Some time into the marriage the architect advised his wife that there was no real future for him in Israel: they had built all their important buildings; all that was left were bus shelters and public lavatories. It was an exaggeration of course, but she got the drift – and did not demur.

So it was that at his instigation they went to Canada. There he thrived and she became a lecturer in Russian at the local university.

She was 'home' on holiday – partly to see her family in Israel and partly to see Shoshana.

But there was one final twist to the story. Shoshana and her friend spoke to each other in Russian – not Hebrew, not Yiddish, not English, not German, but in Russian, the language of their eventful childhood. Speaking Russian as in yesteryear was and is the seal of their unique friendship.

If At First You Don't Succeed ....

Trevor Edward Duncan was known throughout the Ministry of Labour in Scotland as Ted Duncan. Most folk regarded that as an abbreviation of Edward, the name by which he had been known in his days as a student of History at the University of Glasgow.

But that was wrong. In the Civil Service he was known as Ted for these were his initials. Most of his colleagues gave as their initials a scribble which conveyed nothing of any clarity. Duncan wrote slowly but with clarity, and consequently his TED was clear to the world and the world – or at least the department - responded.

'Ted' Duncan finished his career as an Assistant Controller at our Scottish Headquarters in Edinburgh; but when I knew him he was a Senior Executive Officer or a Grade 3 Officer in charge of a large Grade 3 Employment Exchange in the city. I was a mere Grade 5 officer, the lowest position on the Executive scale. At one time I had been on his staff at another Exchange but now we were on the Committee of our Staff Association.

Ted had entered the Department as a cadet. That meant he had been successful in an examination for entry to the Executive grades. Success generally meant 4 or 5 years as a cadet i.e. a sort of half-way house between grade 5 and grade 4. The cadets could generally expect – and experience – promotion in their middle to late twenties to grade 4, after which they were out and running.

One day as we travelled through to Edinburgh for a Committee meeting he told me the story of his candidature.

He had completed his Honours Degree at Glasgow and then, a few weeks later, sat the exam for a cadet-ship. This was not quite as demanding as that for entry to the Administrative grades of the Higher Civil Service.

He did well and was invited to London for interview.

When he was shown into the interview room he was confronted by a long table with a green baize cover and two decanters of water and glasses. Behind the table sat five men and two ladies.

The early questioning was predictable and covered his schooling, his family and his University experience.

Then one of the ladies addressed him.

"Which games do you play?" she asked.

"None," replied Ted.

An awkward silence ensued, but his discomfort was alleviated by a man asking about the quality of the lecturing at Glasgow University.

Ten minutes of further predictable questioning ensued, whereupon a man in his early fifties intervened.

"Tell me, Mr Duncan, which countries, which foreign parts have you visited?"

Ted was inclined to say yet again "None" but thought better of it. He explained he had never been abroad.

It came as no great surprise when he received a letter from the Civil Service Commission advising him that his overall performance had been good — but not good enough.

They thanked him for his interest but concluded by telling him he had not been successful.

Ted was dumped but had seen it coming.

He was of a mind to try again the following year but what to do until then? His family could keep him going or he might pick up a job of sorts. It was then that a friend came to his rescue. His friend, who was studying Medicine and had still a bit to go before graduating, had a father who was a Professor in the History Department. He had a financed research grant and needed three research assistants for a year.

The friend spoke to his dad who indicated he was not averse to having Ted, whom he knew, as one of the three.

Ted worked well and did not displease the historian.

Then he sat the cadet exam. Again he did well and again was invited to attend an interviewing session in London.

When he went down it was the same room, the same table, maybe even the same water. Again there were seven of them; five men and two ladies but a different seven.

It had a gey familiar flavour to it as far as Ted was concerned. The only difference Ted could discern was that the two ladies seemed to be younger and to be wearing more fashionable outfits than the ladies of the previous year had deployed.

There was though a major difference in that Ted was much more prepared.

During the Christmas/New Year vacation he had gone into Partick Public Library and borrowed two books – 'Play Better Golf' and 'How to Holiday in France for Five Pounds a Week'. These he had read thoroughly and had taken copious notes, which had been his bed-time reading the night before the interview.

The early part of the interview went well.

Then one interviewer asked whether he was a 'sporty' type?

Ted said he was certainly not obsessed by sport. As a school boy he had played a little golf. When he became an undergraduate he had resolved to concentrate on his studies, whereupon the clubs had been relegated to the back of the broom cupboard. When he became a researcher he had looked out the clubs and was playing about twice a week. He was enjoying it even though his scoring was at best sad. This observation let to a spirited discussion on the stymie rule, wherein Ted gave a succinct deposition of the case for its retention and that for its curtailment. One of the ladies smiled and said: "I can see you can see both sides of an argument."

Ten minutes later the same lady elbowed her way into the discussion.

"Which countries have you visited?" she asked.

"None," replied Ted but raced on to say "but two of my friends and I are going to France in late July. We believe we can get by on less than five pounds each week."

"Surely not!" exclaimed the lady.

"Oh, yes," said Ted. "We have prepared well. We shall stay in farm houses, sleeping in barns if necessary. We reckon we can live on bread and cheese but we can afford three cheap restaurant meals each week; and of course we shall hitch-hike whenever necessary."

"But surely......" said another panel member taking up the running. Ted dealt most effectively with all their protestations.

"This is fascinating," declared the Chairman, "but we really must stop and let Mr Duncan go. We have other candidates to see."

A few weeks later the Commission wrote to say he had been successful and they, the Commission, were allocating him to the Ministry of Labour.

As observed earlier he finished his career in a very senior position — as an Assistant Controller.

The Excited Father

Miss Primrose Prissy was neither as prim nor prissy as her remarkable nomenclature suggested. True, she was a lady of high moral and religious principles but her lively out-going nature, her interest in others and her highly developed sense of humour showed that a deep Calvinist-based evangelical faith did not inevitably lead to a grim, dull, insular, introspective disposition.

One day she was on a route 31 bus as it travelled south by Mount Florida, King's Park, Simshill, Castlemilk and Carmunnock to East Kilbride. When it stopped near Hampden Park, an un-shaven, badly dressed man joined the bus and elected to sit beside her. As he sat down, he bubbled with enthusiasm.

"Ish it aw-right tae shit ashide ye, missus?" he asked, his saliva spluttering all around him. I think we can take it that his voicing of the main verb was not intentional: he had meant to say 'sit' but what had come out had been totally inadvertent.

Oblivious to this matter he proceeded to confide to his fellow-traveller.

"You shee," he said, "ah'm ferr excited ra day. Ah'm gaun up tae ra Mulk tae shee ma weans. Thish is the day ah get tae shee them, so ah dae."

He paused.

"Ah'm lucky, sho ah um. Ah'v goat thish rare wee burd in Battlefield. But she disnae like me gaun oan an' oan aboot ma weans. Dae ye know, dae ye ken whit she did, sho she did? She hid ma dentures, sho she did!!"

On the Acquisition of Office Furniture

The men – and it was nearly always men – of the 'hard', the 'real' disciplines – disciplines such as Mathematics, Chemistry, Physics, the Classics, Philosophy and the like — did not hold Professor Branton in high regard. Instead, they tended to scoff at him. They saw him as a product of a Commercial College, which was valid as that was what he was, and this not withstanding his three degrees from the University of London.

Then again, it can be argued by way of mitigation that his books had been translated into some ten or twelve languages, nearly all of the Third World. But far from decreasing the criticism, this tended to exacerbate it. His critics argued that many of his books consisted of detail which students in low-level tertiary institutions learned by rote and spewed back at examiners.

I knew him well and knew that this was true of some of his publications, but that there were others which strove to grapple with matters of business, factors and ethics which were examined in demanding fashion.

I recall one of his books on Office Management. One chapter dealt with the basis of setting-up an office and along with other topics dealt with the purchase of office furniture. He listed fourteen points to be considered.

On desks he argued there was a case for ensuring that drawers could be extracted and were not 'fixed' in location. He said that the surfaces should be heat-resistant and – I thought this unduly fussy – that the corners should be rounded off nicely, ensuring that the 'corner' did not consist of right angles. His contention was that this diminished the risk of accidents.

Some years after reading this I found myself in my office, trying to do three different things at the same time, all while expecting an important telephone call.

While I was on a small set of steps, extracting a text-book from the top shelf of a large bookcase, the telephone rang. I jumped from the steps, raced across the floor towards the phone and slammed into the sharp corner of my desk – nearly castrating myself.

Branton was a fuss-pot, but he got more right than he got wrong.

Postscript. It has happened again. Last night I walked into the corner of my wife's dressing table. Ouch!

Assessment by the Guild

By the late sixties my life was rather well-settled. I had been awarded a M.Sc. and a Ph.D. and had been promoted to Senior Lecturer and found an interesting niche in the University. On the domestic front we had moved from a five-apartment house in King's Park to a larger house in Cathcart. On top of all that, a popularised version of my doctoral thesis had been published by Manchester University Press and reviews had been kind.

This acceptable situation left me free to engage in more and more adult education. The two most visible instances of this being two classes for the Extramural Department of the University of Glasgow and even more work than hitherto for the Co-operative Union and the S.T.U.C.

It was the Co-op activity which saw me travelling on a Saturday to Montrose where I was to be the speaker at the quarterly meeting of District Six of the Scottish Co-operative Women's Guild.

Come the day, I was the only male in the hall. The 'body of the kirk' was taken up by some 120 or so delegates gathered in from Tayside to Aberdeen while a platform party consisted of six or seven office bearers – all imposing, all formidable ladies and in particular the very formidable Miss Helib C. Lowe who was the President of the City of Perth Co-operative Society and President of District Six of the Guild.

It was and is one of the many attributes of all branches of the Labour Movement that they not only aspire to but attain very high standards of chairmanship: it is as though their first reading book was Citrine on Chairmanship rather than the Janet and John Book One of their day. The most effective Chairman I ever encountered was the late Willie Bargh of the Glasgow South Society. Miss Lowe ran him a close second.

Exactly on two o'clock she rose and called the meeting to order. She concluded a neat, gracious, succinct message of welcome by announcing the sad passing of Mrs Grant of Forfar Guild: she invited, nay called on us to be 'upstanding' in the memory of Mrs Grant. Chairs scraped the floor as we struggled to rise and then scraped again as we returned to our seats.

Miss Lowe thanked us but as she did so a clear Aberdeen voice cried out "Mrs McGregor o' Aberdeen Sunnybank died a fortnight ago."

Miss Lowe called on us to rise to honour Mrs McGregor.

Again, as we settled, another voice cried out "Mrs Flynn, Dundee Lochee, died twa months ago."

So Helib Lowe had us rise again.

"We lost Miss Sloan of Arbroath twa months ago," cried another voice.

We rose when invited.

"Madam President, you'll remember that we lost Mrs Naughtie of Scone."

Miss Lowe acknowledged her oversight and had us rise again.

And so it went on and on. I stopped counting at twelve but it continued – like the casualties of the first day of the Battle of the Somme.

Eventually it stopped and we turned to the Minutes. Few voluntary organisations, if any, have spent such considerable funding on education as the British Co-op Movement. Yet, even so, many units declined to acknowledge that it had been money well spent and illiteracy had all but gone. So the Minutes were read aloud.

It was all rather predictable until it reached the address by 'the distinguished guest speaker' who, we were told, had been Mr Donald Dewar, "a young and apparently intelligent Member of Parliament". There followed a somewhat lengthy résumé of Donald's speech. Knowing Donald I could recognise some of his phraseology. The account was followed by the observation that questions had been asked by 'Mesdames - ' and then followed a list of names nearly as lengthy as that of the recently deceased.

This was proof positive of a well established Guild practice. By asking a question a delegate was assured of her name appearing in the Minutes, a ploy designed to ensure that one's name became known and thereby increased, however marginally, the chances of being nominated as a delegate to some other activity.

The formidable list of questioners was immediately followed by a *coup de grâce*. It read: "All questions were answered by the speaker, satisfactorily or at least to the best of his ability."

As I listened to such comments I found myself wondering what they would say about me and my speech. I might not have liked it but I would almost certainly have to concede it would be fair. Sychophancy is not in the armoury of the Co-op Guilds.

Mrs Duffy and Mrs Duffy

This is a sad story: indeed, there are those who regard it as a very sad story. That said, it should be reported that there are those who proclaim loudly that they cannot see what the fuss is all about. As they see it, it is an account of a common-place, recurring story of two women who cannot get on with each other but find that relative poverty and family connection have combined to oblige each of them to see more of the other than either would wish.

As the title suggests, both the ladies are called Mrs Duffy. The older lady is the mother-in-law of the younger woman who consequently is the daughter-in-law of the older lady. In the harsh but realistic idiomatic phrase: "There was nae love lost between them".

To follow this story a certain amount of background material is desirable.

Our tale starts in Northern Ireland about the time of the American Civil War, when a family in the heart of the fishing community based in Groomsport on the south-eastern side of Belfast Lough was blessed by the birth of a wee girl. The mother and the father, a man of some standing who owned his own fishing boat, were delighted to have the girl as they already had six sons. The family was called Barron. They were the direct descendants of Scottish fishing families who had been settled in Ulster at the instigation of King James VI and I as part of a scheme to fortify the Province for the Crown and the Reformed Tradition.

The child was called Anna: on the day of the heaviest fighting in the Battle of Gettysburg, Anna Barron came into the world.

When she was seventeen going on eighteen, Anna started going out and about with a boy called John Hannah. John was a

Groomsport lad: he came from Donaghadee which is a few miles along the coast on the road to Bangor. For all that, he was now seen as part of the Groomsport community, not least as he worked on the boats. Originally he had been on one of the boats of the McMillan family, then he moved to a Buchanan boat from which he moved yet again and started sailing on Anna's father's boat. Her father observed that Johnnie, as he called him, was a good worker but was inclined to be sullen.

Then again, the walking out could not be seen as a conventional courtship: he was away too much for that. Sometimes her father and his crew would be away for no more than a handful of days but on other occasions they would be away for weeks running into months. They went, for example, as far as Portugal at least twice each year. Local gossip said that these foreign ventures had more to do with smuggling than they had to do with fishing.

Despite the difficulties Anna and Johnnie married when she was 22 and he was 25.

Sadly, the union never had the outer manifestations of a successful marriage. He was nearly always sullen and ungracious while she was both nervous and glum.

Anna confided in her mother and told her that Johnnie wanted to do 'nasty' things to her but these private conversations never clearly ascertained what was amiss. In part this was due to prudish reticence and partly due to a lack of moderately sophisticated phraseology.

Two years and a bit went by and the place was agog with rumours. Some women asserted that the former Miss Barron was barren while some of John's friends maintained the marriage had never been consummated.

Then there was a dramatic turn of events. Anna's father and three of her brothers came back from ten days' fishing in the Irish Sea and reported to her and to the authorities that John had been swept overboard and must be presumed to be "lost at sea!" And yet, there were those who asserted that he had gone ashore at Stranraer and had subsequently been seen in both Fleetwood and Peel on the Isle of Man.

What was known was that Mr Barron spoke to friends in the Orange Order and his Masonic Lodge and with remarkable alacrity Anna was declared to be a widow.

In the wake of this pronouncement, life for Anna did not change all that much. With Johnnie being away so frequently and sometimes for longish periods, she had spent much of her time back in the family home. With her change of status she gave up the tenancy of the rented cottage where she had spent time with Johnnie when he was ashore. On her return home she took full possession of the bedroom which she had never fully surrendered. Her days were spent on domestic matters as ordained by her mother. For additional company she had Bessie, who was no longer at school. Bessie was not her sister although the entire household treated her as though she was a Barron child. Truth to tell, Bessie was a bit of a mystery. It took years for her full story to emerge. When it did, it became known that on one of the trips to Portugal a matronly local lady brought a two-year-old child to the harbour and threw it into the boat while proclaiming to the world that her daughter was dead, that she had no money and was living in penury and that those who brought this child into the world could and should have her. Then she spat at the boat and hurried away. The inference was that one of the three sons, one of Anna's brothers, was the father.

So it was that the boat returned to Groomsport with an additional person aboard and to her credit Mrs Barron accepted the child and treated her as though she were her own offspring.

About two years after the declaration of widowhood, Anna's life was thrown into total turmoil.

It was a Saturday in high summer and she and two friends had gone into Bangor. When they were buying ice-cream from a vendor at the front, they started chatting to two men in the queue behind them. The men were not elderly or even middle-aged but were not lads. They were in their early thirties.

As they chatted and laughed and as the queue crept forward it became very apparent to the other three that one of the men, the more confident and well-spoken of the two, had taken a shine to Anna and Anna had taken a shine to him.

Anna was in dangerous waters. The man who smiled at her and who laughed or at least smiled at her little jokes had black curly hair which while not a constant hit was nevertheless a recurring characteristic of the indigenous Irish. In other words, it was possible – nay, probable – that he was a Republican and, even worse, a Roman Catholic, a Papist. In short he was likely to be all that she had been brought up to abhor, to fear, to detest.

Oblivious to all of this Anna agreed to meet him the following Saturday.

In all that ensued – and rather a lot was to ensue – Anna never referred to her new friend as a boy-friend. On the contrary she invariably spoke of him by name or as her 'gentleman friend'. On their first outing he introduced himself. His name was Edward Duffy but friends called him 'Eddie'.

To begin with they met, either in Bangor or Belfast, only once a month but that soon moved to fortnightly assignations and then some six months or so after their first encounter to regular weekly events.

The more she saw of him the more she liked what she saw. As she saw it he was a man of knowledge and self-assurance. He used big words. He was well-read and frequently spoke about the book he was reading or one which he had read some time before and she was impressed by the extent he could remember stories he had read many years before. He was confident in dealing with others, treating everyone he encountered as an equal while remaining courteous and considerate. He was not rich yet seemed to be relatively affluent. It transpired that he was a baker to trade but was already a master-baker and as such could produce elaborate cakes such as wedding cakes. As a younger man he had worked in the great Jacob's Bakery in Dublin but had come north to Belfast to live with his two unmarried sisters: they had come north earlier to live with and look after an elderly aunt who lived in a not insubstantial house off the Falls Road.

There was one other matter of import: he neither flaunted nor disguised his Catholicism.

Anna reported much but not all of this to her family.

So it was that for fifteen to eighteen months the courtship – if such it was – continued though it would have been difficult to say progressed. In the theatre at a play or at a concert they would occasionally hold hands and when they were in a park he would sometimes put a protective arm around her but they seldom kissed and when they did it was gey perfunctory.

In due course, however, she was invited to the big house off the Falls Road. The invitation was for 'tea', by inference for high tea.

It did not go well: the sisters were more than a little icy and had not thawed in any way when it came time for Anna's departure.

There was no comparable invitation extended to Edward. Mr Barron, Anna's father, would from time to time throw out his proud declaration that "no known Papist had ever crossed his door." So Anna knew not to raise the matter.

When her parents had learned that the man their daughter was seeing was a Roman Catholic, they did what they could to have her end the relationship. At one point her father considered ordering her to desist but his wife argued that such a course of action could worsen the situation, to which the head of the household queried how it could be worse than it already was.

While this argument proceeded in carousel fashion, Anna came home one Saturday evening sporting an engagement ring.

This development provoked a battery of questions as to where and by whom they were to be married.

It emerged later that at that phase in the proceedings each had chosen to believe that the other would succumb to the expectations of the other.

As it happened, it was Edward and Rome that were to prevail and this was to occur for two reasons. The first was that it was Edward who was the more religious of the two. Anna was not naturally religious: she went to church on Sunday because they all went.

The other reason that Edward triumphed was that he cited the concept and convention which emerged from the religious wars of the 17th century – namely, that a principality should follow the religion of its Prince. If the Prince is Protestant, the Principality should be Protestant and if the Prince is Catholic, the Principality should be Catholic.

Applied to specific couples the convention argues that the young woman should conform and go the road travelled by the young man. If she could not see her way to doing that, she should set about acquiring another prospective husband and he should be one with the same affiliation as herself.

When all of this was put to her by Edward, Anna said she thought that was fair and sensible, indeed, so much so, that she would go further in that not only would she agree to being married by and in the Catholic Church, she would convert and become a Roman Catholic. Edward was a little taken aback at this development but he rallied and proceeded to make arrangements for his fiancée to 'receive instructions' with a view to conversion.

By the time Anna had braced herself and was ready to tell her parents that she was 'receiving instructions' with a view to becoming a Roman Catholic, her father and mother had more than a fair idea as to what she was doing. The local grapevine on lively gossip was as efficient albeit a shade slower than the Bell Telephone system which was destined to descend on the world. So it was that the parents suggested that if she was of a mind to embrace Romanism and all its corrupt activities, then it would be better were she to move out of the house and live somewhere else – presumably with her Papist friends in Belfast; in response, Anna did just that.

Some six months or so thereafter, Edward and Anna were married. Anna had not yet completed her programme of instruction and had not yet been admitted to the Church and so the marriage did not have all the trappings of a Nuptial Mass and Papal Blessing. Instead it was a very simple affair conducted in a monastery off the Falls Road. The brief honeymoon was in Dublin.

****

These events occurred in the middle to late eighties.

On their return from Dublin, the newly-weds set up house in a modest street off the Antrim Road. In due course Anna was received into the Catholic Church. To mark the occasion, Edward arranged for a small party in a parochial hall. His sisters attended but their bodies radiated scepticism and general disapproval.

As the eighties gave way to the nineties Edward and Anna learned that she was pregnant and as they discussed the situation, Anna's Loyalist background shone with the clarity of a lighthouse. She made it abundantly clear that in the event of the child being a girl she wanted it called Victoria and should it be a boy he was to be called Albert after the late Prince Consort.

It was a boy and Albert Duffy made his debut in late June of 1890.

The young family Duffy was destined to spend roughly ten years in the house off the Antrim Road. During the first five years or so things went well for Edward and his wife. She was received into the fold of the Church. She gave birth to Bertie as she called her son and was none the worse for the pains and strains of the pregnancy. Moreover, they were mildly prosperous in that Edward received more overtime than he could cope with comfortably. He was frequently asked by management to produce special cakes for special occasions. He was so accommodating he was known in the management circle as 'Eddie the Ready'. At home, they got on well with their neighbours and the factor.

Then the see-saw tilted. Two families who were close neighbours became quarrelsome while Bertie said his teacher sneered at his name. Worse: an ugly industrial dispute arose in the bakery and Edward found himself articulating the case of the employees. In doing so, he in effect usurped the branch Chairman, an almost incoherent incompetent who had been elected to his post as a result of Masonic influence. The workers prevailed. Edward was rewarded with a noisy round of applause but thereafter incurred the displeasure of both the management and the trade union Chairman and his Masonic backers.

Henceforth, he lost a syllable in that 'Eddie the Ready' and became known as 'Eddie the Red'. He also lost all his overtime and was no longer invited to produce special cakes.

With the continuing deterioration in their fortunes and with their first experience, in their married life, of a shortage of money (having regard to their commitments), Edward pronounced that they would have to do something about it. His first suggestion was that Anna should accept the offer of a part-time job from a local grocer, but Anna made it abundantly clear that she had no intention of taking a job of any sort. She had never been in paid employment and had not the slightest intention of starting, whatever their circumstances. For his part, Edward was surprised at his myopia. Anna, he now realised, was a lady-like buddy and saw herself as at least half a cut above other folk. At the same time he became aware that she was prone to say "After all, my father is a sea captain" as though his fishing boat, while quite large, was a trans-Atlantic vessel taking passengers to the New World or all the way to Australia.

His second suggestion that they should go to Dublin where, he was confident, he would be re-engaged in the large bakery owned by the Jacob family Anna turned down. She did not want to have anything to do with Dublin. Edward reminded her that she had been happy in Dublin when they had been there on their honeymoon. Anna declared that such an observation was irrelevant. So it was he suggested either Liverpool or Manchester but Anna rejected them as being no better than Dublin. She observed that a cousin from Groomsport had gone to Scotland, to Glasgow, and was very happy there. She suggested she should write, did just that and within a month Edward found himself with his wife and child sailing past Ailsa Craig to Glasgow where he was to live, work and die.

****

That day, the day of the arrival of the Duffy family in Glasgow, was to see the introduction of Anna to the realities of working-class life.

Her years in Groomsport had been spent in a 'comfortable' environment and the scattering of months with Johnnie had been quietly subsidised by her mother. Widowhood had seen her return to the family fireplace. The years of courtship and early marriage saw her as a beneficiary of Edward's earning capacity, while their four-apartment house off the Antrim Road saw them as living in a lower middle-class environment and as money grew tighter

Edward put mental emphasis on 'lower' while Anna emphasised the 'middle-class'.

On their arrival at the quay-side in Glasgow they were met by Sarah Cowan, Anna's cousin. Anna had sent some money to her and she had used it to rent a house on their behalf. The modest two-apartment house, referred to locally as a room and kitchen, was on the ground floor off a close in Waddell Street, off the Rutherglen Road. The Cowans lived in Springburn on the north side of town, but Edward had heard good things about the parishes and schools in the prosperous (all things are relative) half of the Gorbals.

Anna was horrified to find they did not have a bathroom and had to share a toilet with the neighbouring family on the other side of the close.

On their first full-day in Glasgow, Edward visited the three big bakers – in Kinning Park, Bridgeton and southern Dennistoun and accepted a job at the Dennistoun Plant. On that day, Anna took Bertie, now 8 years old nearly 9, to the local school of St Francis' Boys. This of course was a parochial school. The Roman Catholic schools were outwith the jurisdiction of the Local Authority until 1918.

Bertie was a tall boy but was not muscular. He did well at St Francis', much better than he did in his Belfast school. He was very good at both Arithmetic and English. This was to be expected as he was a 'bookish' boy who, to his regret, was not proficient at sport.

The 'men' in the family settled to their new roles but Anna resolved she would get a better house. In this quest she was to be successful – but it was to take her twenty years to achieve it.

The twenty years from 1898 to 1918 were years of great importance to the world at large. Motor cars, electricity and the telephone service became common-place, a new alliance was forged between France and the United Kingdom and for more than four years of that period there was the most brutal war the world had ever seen. There had been a Revolution in Russia and an insurrection in Ireland.

All of this had occurred with little apparent effect on the small Duffy family living in their small flat at ground level in Waddell

Street in Glasgow, yet there had been matters which impacted on them at an individual level and which then spilled over and touched the other two.

In the case of Edward nothing appeared to change. He worked away for all twenty years in the bakery in South Dennistoun. But his situation had changed and his confidence eroded with the result that his buoyancy was visibly reduced. All of this arose in the wake of his having been taken aside by one of the managers and told that they saw him as a competent employee; accordingly they were ready to go on employing him, but word of his trade union militancy had crossed the Irish Sea, so they were warning him that on the slightest indication of trouble they would find some plausible reason for sacking him. Furthermore, he could forget about promotion: there would be none for him. On that front his Catholicism did not help; on the contrary, it was a positive handicap.

Thereafter Edward was a much more subdued man. His ebullience had gone. His cocky disposition disappeared.

In the case of Anna there was quite a different change. Young boys are notoriously unobservant but even Bertie noticed that his mother was missing Mass rather frequently. There is a passage in the Bible when folk who have been invited to a wedding decline to attend observing "I have married a wife" or "I have bought two oxen" but Anna's excuses were more prosaic. One Sunday she maintained she had "a cold coming on". Another Sunday she had a severe headache and on yet another, that her leg was very sore or even that she did not feel like it.

Eventually she bit the bullet and told Eddie that she now realised she had made an awful mistake in adopting Catholicism. Truth to tell, she just did not believe it. She had done it to please him and she was of a mind to return to the Presbyterian fold of her parents. Edward did not argue: instead he accepted it with commendable equanimity.

The biggest and most readily visible change in the small Duffy family was in Bertie, who grew from a shy, reticent boy of eight years to a full-grown, mature and moderately confident man working his way towards his thirties.

The twenty-year run started well for him in that he took to and responded well to his new school. Fortunately, the school responded well to him. He was clever and bright, albeit not the best boy in his year. He did what he was told, he worked hard and always did his homework. Like almost all working-class boys of the first decade of the new century he was fated to leave school at the age of fourteen, when his final report card recorded that he was particularly good at Arithmetic, English and Religious Knowledge. All of this was fortified by quite outstanding handwriting. The school authorities in the 'obiter dicta' went on to say that many of his attributes were liable to be fortified as he was an avid reader.

On leaving school he obtained employment as an office boy and when he was sixteen moved to a post as a trainee solicitor's clerk with a legal firm in West Regent Street. Throughout these years he attended evening classes and obtained certification in Shorthand, Book-keeping and Business Practice. He found his work to be congenial and well within his competence and he revelled in finding a free fifteen or twenty minutes of his lunch-time and slipping out of the office to rummage through the books on the book barrows which were to be found in that part of town.

At home in his parish he did not serve in any capacity in the church. Similarly, he did not join the Boys' Guild. Nevertheless at 22 or 23 he joined the Young Men's Society and when he was 24 and about the August of 1914 and the outbreak of war he joined the Knights of Saint Columba and started attending diverse events in the range of Parochial Halls in Errol Street. It was there that he met and got to know Kate Moran – and life was never the same again.

Kate Moran was exactly what Bertie Duffy needed. She introduced him to a wide range of activities in the Parochial Halls and in other halls in the vicinity. She was lively without being noisy and gregarious. She made friends easily and having admitted them to friendship kept them

There was another factor here. The Morans were a fairly big family: there were seven of them in addition to the mother and father. They were active in the affairs of the parish, both religious and social.

One of her sisters, Mary, was a natural organiser and not only arranged for Sunday charabanc outings to Waterfoot, Eaglesham, East Kilbride and the like, but summer holidays to Portrush and Cushendun, both in Northern Ireland.

The overall effect of all this was that Bertie found himself being caught up in most, if not quite all, these activities.

Moreover, whereas there was never a formal proposal, there arose an understanding that in the fullness of time – whatever that meant – Bertie and Kate would get married. The war started in August 1914 just as they and their friends were returning from Portrush and by the end of the first year of activities the Bertie/Kate situation was recognised and accepted by all their friends.

Bertie did not volunteer for military service although many of his friends did. Eventually conscription was introduced and Bertie was 'called up'. He was not a robust young man and it came as no surprise when he was classified as Grade C yet called to the colours. He was assigned to a Field Service Unit to undertake general duties of the kind later undertaken by the Pioneer Corps in the Second World War.

Somebody pointed out that were they to get married Kate would get a modest allowance and were he to be killed, a war widow's pension. So it was that in November 1917 they were married in the great St Francis Church in Cumberland Street.

It was not without significance that Bertie wore a suit and not his uniform.

And, of course, Kate became a Mrs Duffy – much to Anna's annoyance.

****

The Great War, as it came to be called, came to its dramatic end at eleven o'clock on the eleventh day of the eleventh month of 1918 but Bertie was not released until the following spring.

He was not long home until the young couple were confronted with two serious problems.

The first arose when he called at his law firm in the city centre fully expecting to resume his employment. The senior partner explained, in none too gentle terms, that another young man who had been deemed to be Grade 4 and so not called to the Services was doing the job and doing it so well and at lower cost to the firm. There was no opening for Bertie. They would give him good references provided he was not difficult.

Bertie observed that it was his understanding that Government Regulations made it clear that ex-service personnel were to be reinstated in their pre-service employment. The senior partner's response to this was to observe that it was being honoured in the breach. Bertie said he could appeal to a Tribunal, an observation to which the employer asserted that Bertie could take them to the Tribunal but that were he to do so he would lose and say good-bye to the good references.

Bitterly disappointed, Bertie discussed the situation with Kate who, having great confidence in his ability, advised her husband to grab the good references and seek alternative employment.

Two weeks later he was engaged as a cashier/book-keeper in a large licensed grocery establishment in Hamilton. The wage was not great but the post entitled him to the occupancy of a flat above the shop. A further two weeks on he started work and he and Kate took up residence in their new home.

The other problem proved to be Bertie's health. When he was demobilised Bertie was said to have a bad cold. It seemed to persist through the summer months and by October his doctor in Hamilton referred him to a quasi-specialist, who after conducting a very detailed examination, looked grave and pronounced that Bertie had a severe bronchial condition almost certainly caused by the conditions, both in work and in tented accommodation while with the Army in France.

The spell in Hamilton for Bertie and Kate lasted about two and a half years.

Both the town and the flat were pleasant enough and he found the work interesting and well within his competence but they both missed Glasgow and what it had to offer. To be honest, neither missed the parents: fortnightly trips into town to see the parents were enough. Bertie, however, missed the rummaging at book-barrows and the range of stock in the bigger book-shops. In addition, he missed the general 'buzz' of the place and not least the clanging of the tram-cars. As for Kate, her sense of loss was greater. She missed the events in the Parochial Halls and the wide range of friends she met there. As well, she missed her sisters and brothers although the feminine loss was the greater of the two.

So it was they returned to town, to a room and kitchen, two-apartment flat in Cumberland Street in the heart of the St Francis parish.

****

At much the same time Anna and Edward left the house in Waddell Street and took occupancy of another room and kitchen house on the top floor of a close in Hutcheson Square. This house had two advantages which warranted the move. Firstly, it had an internal toilet and, secondly, it looked out over a children's swing park which, in turn, was surrounded with trees. Trees were very rare in the Gorbals and Anna took an almost proprietorial pride in being able to see them as and when it took her fancy which was quite frequently — on ever day the Good Lord sent to her.

Obtaining the two houses – that of the younger couple in Cumberland Street and that of his parents in Hutcheson Square – was not difficult. At that time every other close had a board outside it indicating that the Factor had a house to let. Given that a potential tenant was willing to pay the weekly rent requested, entry was well-nigh assured. Haggling, negotiating over the marginal threepence or sixpence was almost always of no avail.

Finding employment for Bertie was markedly more difficult. Openings for solicitors' clerks were virtually non-existent while those for book-keepers and cashiers were few and far between. In due course Bertie realised he would have to settle for a less prestigious post, and a lower salary, therefore less money than he had been earning (having regard to the hidden saving of the rent-free flat in Hamilton).

Eventually he became an 'agent' for the Household Supply Company which was a large, almost impressive, furniture warehouse

133

on the London Road, not far from Glasgow Cross. Customers received their purchase on credit which was subjected to interest at a rather high rate. Bertie's duty was to call weekly or fortnightly to uplift these contributions towards paying off the debt. Further purchases were refused until the debt had been cleared.

This employment involved climbing tenement stairs and being out and about in some dreadfully inclement weather.

It was most unsuitable work for a man with a severe bronchial condition – but it was a job.

Two other events of considerable importance were to impact on the Duffy family.

In 1925 Kate gave birth to a boy. No-one was surprised when Anna suggested, indeed assumed, that the boy be called Albert, but the young couple was for none of it and named him Francis, in recognition of the saint in whose church the boy was baptised on the Sunday following his birth.

Later that same year Edward took a shock. He never worked again. When he was released from hospital he came home to a large cot bed which was erected in the kitchen. To her credit, Anna looked after him magnificently. She had been and still was wife and house-keeper. To these roles was added that of nurse and she had to be a nurse on constant duty – twenty four hours a day, seven days a week. This she did, without a single word of complaint, for four years and more until he died in the closing days of 1929.

The two Duffy households, living in comparative proximity, staggered through the early thirties.

Following Edward's death the family in Groomsport suggested that Anna, Bertie, Kate and wee Frank should all come for a holiday in Groomsport. Notwithstanding a decided lack of enthusiasm on Kate's part, they went to Ulster for the Glasgow Fair fortnight of 1930. In one sense this was unfortunate as they arrived in the wake of the local holiday celebrations marking the anniversary of the 1690 Battle of the Boyne in which encounter William III had a glorious victory over the Irish forces backed by the French. Every year in Northern Ireland the Protestant community, particularly those of the 'Scots-Irish' community, celebrated the event and chose to ignore the fact that in 1690 the Pope had been supporting William and, on hearing of his victory called for the singing of a *Te Deum* in the Vatican.

Wee Frank was very taken with the red, white and blue bunting decorations on all the boats including his grandfather's. The day of major celebration was past but the bunting was left in situation for some time thereafter. It was the only memory Frank was to have of Groomsport and of his relatives who lived there.

As the Groomsport holiday was coming to a close the Barron family chaffed, conned Anna into agreeing to take her brother Samuel back with her to her house in Glasgow. Samuel was the least endowed of the six brothers. His employment record was, at best, somewhat haphazard. From time to time he was assigned the task of tidying up the boat but, as often as not, he left the craft in worse condition rather than in better 'nick'. He was unmarried. No local maiden had been sufficiently foolhardy as to regard him as suitable marital material.

Despite these and other visible deficiencies the argument advanced by the others was that he would constitute 'company' for Anna, particularly on the long winter evenings. It was also observed that his pathetic shillings from the forerunner of the National Assistance Board would contribute towards the income flow of the household, an argument which ignored the cost of having him.

In those days of the early thirties there were 'little incidents' which strained the Anna-Kate relationship. Most of the these matters eventually faded from memory, though their effect remained. Two of them, however, stayed in the minds of the family. One was known as the Craigmore incident, the other as the matter of the pedal-car.

In 1931 the Morans were holidaying in Bute. They had rented a rather fine house. Kate and Frank were to be there for a month while Bertie was to be there for two weeks.

Mrs Moran suggested that Bertie's mother should be invited for a day. Bertie wrote conveying the invitation and nominating the date and giving explicit instructions on travel.

It all went wrong and became known as 'The Craigmore Incident'. This arose from the fact that Rothesay had two piers. The first of these was the big busy bustling harbour in Rothesay — which pier is still with us. In those days there was also a pier at Craigmore to the south of town. It was a much smaller, quieter, almost sedate pier. Access to Rothesay Pier was one penny and there was a charge for coming off. Access to Craigmore cost fourpence – two pence to go on it and another two pence to leave it. In writing to his mother Bertie had advised her to come off the boat at Rothesay where he, Kate and Frank would be there to meet her. He had told her the time of the train from St Enoch in Glasgow, when it reached Wemyss Bay and when the boat would leave Wemyss Bay and when it would arrive at Rothesay.

Come the day Bertie and his wife and boy were on the Pier to meet and greet her but there was no Anna. They waited for another boat from Wemyss Bay to arrive but there was still no Anna. Thereupon they returned to the big house to see if there had been any word. They were both surprised and put out to find Anna sitting by the fire, drinking tea and eating scones. What had happened? She had left the boat at Craigmore. 'Someone' had said this was Rothesay. She had seen big houses and took it this was where the Morans were staying. And as to how she got from the Pier to the house – she had known her Bertie would want her to take a taxi and she was sure he would pay for it. Bertie compensated her though he could ill afford it.

****

Anna's cousin, who lived on the north side of Glasgow and who had been instrumental in the Duffys obtaining the house in Waddell Street, had three sons, one of them working as a janitor in a primary school in much the same district. As janitor he had the tenancy of a large, fine red-sandstone house in the grounds of 'his' school. He had taken his mother to live with him and his family.

Anna visited this lady about six times a year. The janitor had a son, known within the family as 'Boy Blue'. He, the boy, was much of an age with Frank.

On one occasion the cousin suggested that Anna should bring Frank and the boys could play together in the wide, open schoolyard after 4 o'clock of an afternoon when the school-day was finished and the pupils had gone home. The boys could have the yard to themselves.

So it was that Anna would collect Frank and they would travel on the white tram-car all the way from Crown Street to Springburn.

'Boy Blue' was the proud owner of a flashy, bright pedal-car. Frank was to find that 'playing in the yard' consisted of his standing cold and forlorn while 'Boy Blue' pedalled furiously around the yard. Frank was never offered 'shots' — however brief — on the car. So far as 'Boy Blue' and his parents were concerned, being allowed to watch 'Boy Blue' should have been pleasure and privilege enough. Anna had not remonstrated.

A further factor was that Kate found that she resented the way Anna had converted to Catholicism and then discarded it.

According to Anna she had adopted Roman Catholicism "to please her Edward" but found that "it did not suit her".

Kate knew she was no zealous Catholic but she thought it wrong and unbecoming to adopt a religion – any religion – on such thin grounds and then to discard it as one would discard a dress which no longer pleased her.

When she discussed it with Bertie he took the view that his mother had acted in good faith. More, he argued, it would have been more wrong of her to stay with Catholicism when her heart was not with it.

But Kate persisted with her more critical view.

That evening things were rather cool in the young Duffy household.

****

For all that, the decade of the thirties was to prove to be one of success and frequent spells of happiness for the family.

In 1934 not one but two pieces of good fortune came their way. The first of them concerned Bertie who succeeded in obtaining employment as a clerk in an Employment Exchange in the East End of the city. This had two great advantages. Firstly, it saved him from trachling through the town in all sorts of inclement weather. The second advantage was that the annual salary was much better than in his job as an agent.

The other piece of good fortune was their being allocated a ground floor, three-apartment Corporation house in Riccarton Street, Govanhill. The original idea had been that Anna would join them but the presence of Samuel negated that plan. That said, Kate was mightily relieved.

In 1936 more good fortune came their way when Frank was awarded a scholarship to a prestigious school in the city centre.

War was declared on Sunday 3rd September 1939 and Kate and every other British mother of a teenage boy shivered. A week and a day later, Samuel Barron died. Before the week was out he was buried. These were the days when only men attended the cemetery for the internment and it was a gey sparse collection who gathered round the grave. Anna had returned to the burning bush of the Church of Scotland and her minister officiated despite the fact that Samuel never attended that or any other church.

In the weeks following his demise there was a long, protracted debate on whether Anna should give up the house in Hutcheson Square and join Bertie, Kate and Frank in Riccarton Street. The hidden factor here, a factor that was never voiced, was that the ladies did not like each other. Anna did not approve of Kate and regarded her as not good enough for Bertie whose Barron grandfather owned his own boat whereas Kate's father was "just a fireman" on the engines of the Glasgow and Western Railway. Seen from Kate's end of the telescope Anna was pretentious, always suggesting that she was superior to others, particularly the Morans, and this despite the fact that the two unmarried sisters had bought a small four-apartment house in Boyd Street. Another matter which irritated Kate was that Anna steadfastly refused to join the local Co-operative Society, preferring, instead, to shop in a wee shop and knowingly pay prices above those of the Coop. Asked why she did this she explained that the shop-owner recognised her as a lady and treated her as such.

Initially it was decided that Anna should sail alone and that Kate, who was a very economic housewife, would subvent her by giving her the odd ten shillings or a pound. By early 1942, however, it became clear that Anna was failing and she was brought into the fold of Bertie's household.

Here it should be noted that the three-apartment Corporation houses were at one and the same time very good houses and very bad houses. The difficulty was that the big room to the front of the house was neither a natural bedroom nor was it a natural public room.

The Duffy family had gone for a different approach. The room to the back of the house was regarded by most tenants as the living room, an approach fortified by the fact that it had a coal fire which heated the tank which stored the hot water, particularly during the war when coal was the sole source of heating for the house. There was a coal fireplace in the big room but it was seldom used. The view had been taken that Bertie needed all the heat he could obtain and as a consequence he and Kate slept in a bed settee in the living room while young Frank slept in a conventional bed in the big room.

When Anna arrived she acquired occupancy of the big room while Frank retreated to the third room, a small bedroom which had a broken gas fire which the Gas Department claimed could not be repaired as the parts were not available because of the war.

So our long story works its way towards its conclusion. The eventful years here were those from 1942 until 1945 though so far as 1942 was concerned the salient events were packed into the last two months of that year.

In early November Bertie went off sick with yet another severe attack of bronchitis. In the third week of that spell he rose late and went into the bathroom to shave. While there he took a severe, alarming fit of coughing and dropped dead. He was 52. His G.P., an undistinguished product of the Anderson School of Medicine (fated to be abolished at the end of the war), attributed the death to a heart attack associated with protracted bronchitis and consequential coughing. Understandably, Anna took the death very badly. As she observed to her minister, Mr Templeton: "It is a terrible thing for a mother to see her only child in his coffin".

As though Bertie's death were not bad enough, three weeks later Frank who was then eighteen received his call-up papers instructing him to report to the Army.

So over the ensuing Christmas and New Year the Duffy household in Riccarton Street was reduced to two. That in itself was distressing but their financial position added to their plight. The two salary earners had gone as had their incomes. Kate assessed the situation which was gey bleak. Their income flow was the pathetic pensions and an allowance from Frank's modest Army pay to his mother.

To all of this Kate's solution was to get a job and take a lodger. She found both. She was taken on as a school dinner lady and allocated to St Francis' School which she knew well. She found her lodger in a Mr Marley who was employed as a bar manager by a company with over sixty pubs in Scotland and the North of England. He lived in Edinburgh but had been appointed as manager to the company's third largest bar which was in the centre of Glasgow.

Together these moves alleviated the financial situation but one knock-on effect was that Anna had to surrender the big bright room with the fire and take the pathetic wee bedroom with the broken gas fire which had been occupied by Frank. All this left unanswered the matter of where Frank would sleep as and when he came home on leave. As Kate saw it there were two possibilities: either he could sleep on a camp-bed in the lobby or he could stay with his aunts in their house in Boyd Street.

Mr Marley was a well-nigh perfect lodger. He arose at a time which fitted in well with the movements of the two ladies. Kate rose early, cleared the bathroom, wakened Anna and saw her into the bathroom. While she was there, Kate made breakfast for the two of them and after that somewhat frugal meal saw to the two beds. Anna would go back to her new freshly made bed and having seen to the bed settee, Kate restored the room to its living room status. Her next tasks were to waken Mr Marley and prepare his breakfast while he shaved and washed and as he ate and read the morning newspaper, she tidied his room. This involved clearing and resetting the fireplace in that room. During the programme of her earlier tasks she had to find time to see to the fireplace in the living room.

Mr Marley left for his bar as soon as he finished his breakfast whereupon Kate washed all the breakfast dishes and put them away in the cupboard. Shortly thereafter she would make a fresh pot of tea. After the tea she would prepare a lunch tray for Anna and make sure she had the newspaper, her library book and her magazine — which was usually *The People's Friend* — and tell her what was coming up on the radio. Then she left for the school and would do her shopping on her way back home.

It was usually between four o'clock and quarter past four when Kate returned home from school and her subsequent shopping although she could be later if she had met a talkative neighbour.

It is significant that while the white tram-car from the Gorbals to her most convenient stop in Govanhill would have cost her a penny, Kate did not avail herself of that arrangement. Being economical she took the tram up the hill to the fare stage at Aikenhead Road which journey cost her a half-penny. At that point she left the tram and walked the rest of the way, doing so just as the hill levelled out to a virtual plateau. This arrangement enabled her to save tuppence-halfpenny a week. That was in old money. In contemporary money it would be about one penny a week.

Once she was in the house she made a pot of tea for Anna and herself and lit the fire. She then devoted the better part of an hour to domestic chores such as washing, ironing and dusting or going over such carpets as they had with her poor little Ewbank sweeper. When five struck it generally found her making an evening meal for Anna, which meal she served at the table in the living room. Whatever her other attributes, Kate was no great cook. These midweek meals generally involved a frying pan: it was only at the weekend that she ventured into what other folk would call real cooking. When Anna had finished eating, Kate would wash and put away the dishes. She would see Anna sitting in a big arm-chair by the side of the fire and remind her of the programmes coming up on what they both called the wireless, whereupon she would leave to go to her sisters' house in Boyd Street where she made the evening meal for them, their unmarried brother who lived with them, and for herself.

Following that meal she would generally spend much of the evening with them but almost always rise by nine o'clock to go back to her own house – and Anna. At ten o'clock she made tea and two small sandwiches and the two of them ate and chatted through until about half-past the hour when Anna retired to bed. At about quarter to eleven Mr Marley arrived in from his bar and looking for his evening meal. Kate would busy herself in the kitchen while Mr Marley had the privacy of the living room to eat his meal, read his evening paper and smoke his last cigarette of the day. Once Mr Marley had cleared the bathroom and said good-night and retired to his own room, Kate would again see to the dishes, rake the pathetic fire, clear the bathroom, say her prayers, adjust the bed settee whereupon the living room became a bedroom until the next morning.

Given that account of day-to-day life in the Duffy household one might quite easily be lured into thinking all was well in the Duffy household.

But it wasn't.

The apparent civilities were not just a façade but an extremely thin veneer of amicable living. The exchanges between the two ladies had all the sincerity of the handshake of two football managers at the end of a particularly acrimonious and bitter match.

It had never been a good relationship. The ladies did not like each other. Each was resentful of the other.

Kate was troubled in conscience. She oscillated considerably. At times she told herself that she was doing all she could for her mother-in-law. On other occasions she rebuked herself for not doing more for her. One recurring matter of self-rebuke was when she acknowledged that she did not need to spend as long as she did in Boyd Street. On other occasions she congratulated herself for doing as well as she did. For example, she went out of her way to produce as fine a tea as rationing would allow for the Saturday afternoon when Anna's minister, Mr Templeton, called to see her. What Kate did not know was that when Anna told Mr Templeton she felt neglected and unappreciated, the minister pointed out that in one sense she was fortunate in that were she not to be with Kate she would be in some home or other and he knew from other visitations how dreadful some them could be. Anna who knew her Bible did not argue with Mr Templeton but when he had gone she would wonder why he did note Ruth who, as Anna chose to see it, had capitulated entirely to her mother-in-law.

This uneasy relationship continued as the war progressed. Neither of them was happy yet neither gave voice to her disquiet – other than to Mr Templeton and to Kate's confessor.

Then, quite suddenly, without forewarning Anna died.

She died on the day of the disastrous Arnhem landing, the day on which Frank's glider crashed on landing, the day on which Frank was both seriously injured and taken as a prisoner of war.

At Anna's funeral there was a sparse gathering of men. The janitorial son of her cousin on the north side of Glasgow was there. At the ensuing 'reception' for the mourners it transpired that no-one from the Barron side, neither in Groomsport nor in Glasgow, was in the Forces, but many were prospering in war work. At that time all Kate knew about Frank was that he was 'missing'.

Kate realised that she would now be on her own, apart from the support of her sisters and brother, all the while praying that Frank would return safe and sound. Kate was destined to live until her late eighties, during which she had her memories, not least those of her relationship with her mother-in-law, the other Mrs Duffy.

An Event on a Subway

It should be admitted that in the telling of these stories the references to time are, on occasion, not wrong but rather imprecise. When I say, "it happened in the mid seventies", it covers a five-year period running from high summer of 1972 to the same season in mid-1977.

That said, in this story the situation is markedly more precise.

It happened on an evening in the late summer of either 1960 or 1961. I do not know which but I am certain it was one or t'other.

My wife and two daughters were in Largs. Like many other families we had rented a seaside house for a month. I had my fortnight's holiday and went down for the other weekends but for the non-Largs working days I was residing in our house in King's Park in Glasgow and my day was spent working in an Employment Exchange in the north-west sector of town.

On the evening in question I was doing a little overtime and had been invited by our friends Ralph and Beryl McGuire to join them in their house in Pollokshields for my 'tea'. A high tea, of course. In other words, an evening meal.

On the evening concerned I worked till after 6.30 and caught a tram-car which had me at St George's Cross just before 7 o'clock.

My intention was to take an underground train. The Glasgow underground system – affectionately called the 'subway' — is the only such system in the UK outside London. It is a simple circle, a gey rough circle where the trains run in opposite directions. I planned to travel from St George's Cross, the most northerly station, to Cessnock, the most southerly of the stations. From Cessnock I would walk through Bellahouston to Pollokshields and the McGuire house.

While I was waiting on the platform of the subway station I sensed that the place was a shade busier than I had expected but did not give it a second thought. At Kelvinside Station more folk got on than alighted and this proved to be even more true at Hillhead.

It was when we reached Partick that I realised what was happening. At this station the situation was markedly busier than usual. Moreover, the crowd was predominately male and many of them were wearing Rangers scarves. All fell into place: Rangers were due to play that night in a European competition. Hence the crowd.

If all this was true of the Partick scene its validity became ever more apparent when we reached Govan Cross. There the platform was thronged. The carriages of our train were now fully utilised. Every seat was taken and every inch of standing room was occupied. The conductor, not a native of these shores, had apparently emanated from somewhere in the substantial Indian sub-continent. Dressed in his green Glasgow Corporation uniform he had immediately incurred the antipathy of the blue-clad horde.

He called aloud for his travellers to move up the carriages. Those to whom he directed his request did not respond well to his exhortation. Instead, an avalanche of abuse descended on him. His geographic and ethnic origins were thoroughly denounced. His parentage was abused. His size – he was not very big – was despised. Every foul term – nouns, adjectives, adverbs and verbs – was deployed.

At last we arrived at Copeland Road station, the nearest station to the Rangers' stadium.

As the doors opened there was an eruption – indeed two! Firstly, there was a sound with an element of relief broadly akin to a very large elephant breaking wind. Then the people made their way towards the exit stairs.

One wee man, a dapper well-groomed wee man, joined the train but went into the other carriage.

My carriage was now occupied by two of us – a very well-dressed elderly lady of settled, proper disposition and me.

The lady dusted something from her coat and smiled over at me.

"An awful lot of people," she ventured.

"Yes, indeed," I replied.

"It makes you wonder where they are all going, doesn't it?" she suggested.

"Ibrox," I replied.

The lady's whole frame shook in restrained delight.

"Oh," she said. "Is Billy Graham back in Glasgow?"

The Afrikaans Paper

During the 39-45 war those of us in the Royal Air Force and the Fleet Air Arm who had volunteered for aircrew duties (i.e. flying duties), found that we were destined to be sent to the USA or various parts of what was still called 'The Empire' to do some of our training. Canada, South Africa and Rhodesia saw many of them. All of this was particularly true of those of us who aspired to be pilots, navigators and bomb aimers, our training being longer than that of other aircrew activities. Irrespective of destination, we were well-nigh assured of generous hospitality.

I went to South Africa and I can well remember the quite wonderful hospitality my friend George Cannon and I received from a family called Morley who lived in a spacious bungalow near the beach at Port Elizabeth. The Morleys had a daughter of much the same age as ourselves and a son who was a few years younger. They were a delightful family and were extremely generous in their hospitality.

Later, when I was stationed in East London, also in the Cape Province, another RAF man and I went to Grahamstoun invited there for a long weekend to the home of two late middle-aged ladies. They I think were called Burroughs. I do remember that one was called Enid and the other Emily – a situation which caused confusion when mail arrived addressed to 'Miss E. Burroughs'.

Towards the end of my period in South Africa a tall lad from Leicester – he claimed his father was an entrepreneur and owner of a ladies-stockings factory – joined me in receiving the hospitality of a Cape Town family called Lorimer. Most of this occurred in a fine house in suburbia, but extended to a 'holiday' house by the sea, a few miles beyond the British Naval Base at Simonstown on the Cape Peninsula. It was a white-washed house with five or six bedrooms. I remember we spent one day fishing for sharks. I remember, too, seeing thumb and other finger-prints on the wall by the windows. Foolishly, I observed that they should not allow their grand-children to climb the wall and enter by the bedrooms. To this, their response was to laugh and point out that the prints were those of a baboon which lived on the hills of the peninsula.

One member of their extended family was a young man called Stewart Lorimer who had fairly recently graduated from the local university.

He had sat the examination for entry to the higher ranks of their Civil Service.

He had done well but not well enough in that he had done very well in every paper, with one exception: he had failed in Afrikaans, when success in both languages, English and Afrikaans, was a *sine qua non* for entry to the Service.

Disappointed, but not too put out, he resolved to tackle the 're-sit' some five months later. For that period he put away his golf, tennis and surfing material. He devoted all his time to working on his Afrikaans. He read, he listened to tapes, he conversed in Afrikaans with some bi-lingual accomplices.

Come the day of the re-sit exam he was not confident but assured his anxious parents that he knew he was better prepared than he had been at the time of the first attempt.

Yet, within two minutes of the commencement of the exam, he knew his endeavour had been to no avail. Yes, he was better equipped than he had been first time round, but the paper was decidedly more demanding that that of his earlier attempt. He thought this most unfair. The second exam paper he reckoned should have been of the same severity of its predecessor. In disgust he crumpled the exam paper, the answer book and the virginal blotting paper into one large paper-ball and deftly drop-kicked the lot into a large waste paper bin.

The atmosphere at home that evening was 'difficult'.

Some weeks later while he was walking aimlessly in Adderley Street in Cape Town another young man whom he knew slightly stopped him and said: "I just wanted to congratulate you on passing your Afrikaans. That will be you going into the Higher Civil Service, will it not? Congratulations. Saw the good news in the *Cape Times*. Well done, old man, well done."

Stunned, Stewart bought the paper and went into a café for a coffee. There it was in black and white. An introductory passage observed that the Civil Service Authorities had announced the result of the re-sit exams. A healthy team of Afrikaaner names had passed in English and a smaller team of British names had passed in Afrikaans. And, lo, there he was – Lorimer, S.T.

But how? He had not put pen to paper.

What to do? He did not take the train home. He walked and gave thought to his situation.

By the time he put his key in the door of his home, Stewart had come up with a plan of action which he hoped, indeed believed, would lead to a solution which would reconcile both his conscience and his aspirations for a successful career.

He had resolved he would go and see his former English master, the Rev. Dr. Christopher Middlemass at his grammar school, a fee-paying 'faith school'. Dr. Middlemass was acting Headmaster as the regular Head was in hospital.

Two or three days later he was back in the school and with Dr. Middlemass who, the situation having been reported by Stewart, puffed on his pipe and looked thoughtful.

"How many candidates were there?" he asked.

"About 23 or 24," replied Stewart.

"And how many passed?" asked the master.

"Fifteen," said Stewart.

Dr. Middlemass looked thoughtful.

"Hmmm," he hummed. Then he put his pipe down and put his fingers together.

"My theory, my likely explanation," he observed, "is that an examiner was sent all the scripts and a list of candidates with a column for the insertion of the marks. On completion of the marking he started transcribing the marks to the schedule – and found to his horror he was one short. He hunted everywhere but did not find it. What would he do? Rather than admit he was one short, I reckon he would give the missing script the sort of mark an indifferent candidate would score on a good day and which a relatively good candidate would obtain on a bad day – 56 seems very likely. So I suggest two things. Firstly, you accept the post. You are almost certain to be appointed to a predominately English speaking area and you can improve your Afrikaans as you go along. My second suggestion is that I write to the Civil Service in my capacity as Acting Head and say that I know it is highly irregular but could they let me know your score. I shall suggest that we here are doing a survey of our young men and their prospective careers."

He lifted his pipe again, struck a match and puffed at the pipe.

"Agreed?" he asked – and to be fair, it was more a question than it was a declaration.

"Agreed," replied Stewart, who then rose and thanked his former tutor and made for the door.

As he did so, Dr. Middlemass rose and said: "I shall phone you, Stewart. Soon, I hope."

A week went by and it was a long week for Stewart but one night as dinner was about to be served, the phone rang. His father answered it and then called: "Stewart! Dr. Middlemass for you."

Stewart took the phone and announced himself.

"Fifty-five, Stewart, fifty-five," said the master and went on: "Accept the post. The system has decreed it. And God bless you and your family. Good night."

As we were sailing to Blighty Stewart Lorimer was embarking on his Civil Service career – in Cape Town, a predominantly English-speaking city.

En Route to the Semi-Final

It would be most unfortunate were the ladies and some men to be put off this story because it is about football. Such folk should be reassured. There will be no ball kicked, no goal scored, no whistle blown, no cards flashed: the story deals with the journey to the game.

The incident occurred in the early fifties. I cannot be certain but as I recall it there was to be a replay of a semi-final of a cup competition. The two teams had played in an intriguing game on the Saturday, but it had ended in a 2-2 draw. Now on the ensuing Wednesday they were due to play again.

I was keen to attend but to do so I had to get away early from my post at Bridgeton Employment Exchange. My supervisor was a local man who was a Clyde supporter and was sympathetic to my aspiration and we agreed that I would come in at 8.30 on two mornings and could slip away at 4 o'clock on the day of the replay.

But how to get from Bridgeton to Hampden? There was no direct public transport and even if there had been it would have been swamped.

So what to do? My solution was to go to Bridgeton Cross and endeavour to 'hitch-hike' a lift on one of the many supporters' buses easing their way through that six-street intersection.

I was lucky. It did not take long for me to be successful.

A bus drew in and the folding door opened. A cheeky-looking man was standing on the top step.

"Gaun tae ra gemme, son?" he enquired.

I said I was.

"A' right, oan ye come," he cried and as I climbed the three steps, he continued, "there's wan seat right at the very back. Take that wan."

I did as directed.

When I reached the back there was indeed a seat next to a small, shirpit, somewhat sleekit wee man in the corner.

As I sat down and merely nodded to him, he sat up and seemed to recognise me.

"It's yersel!" he declared.

I agreed.

"Aye, ah thought it was you," he revealed. Silence prevailed but not for long.

"You'll be busy," he declared.

"Yes, we're always busy," I replied.

At this he stirred himself.

"Aye, ye will be," he concurred.

This inconsequential exchange continued for a while but the longer it went on, the more it became apparent to me that we were at cross-purposes. I said just that.

The wee man looked both perplexed and annoyed.

"But you're a screw at the Bar-L, ur ye no'?" he asked.

"No," I said. "I'm not a warden at Barlinnie," I observed.

"Well, did ye used tae be wan?" he asked.

"No – never," I declared with an adamant tone.

"Well, if ye are no' a screw, whit dae ye dae?" he asked.

"I'm on the staff at Bridgeton Employment Exchange," I explained.

"Ah – the Buroo," he echoed.

"Yes," I said.

"Aye, right enough, I knew you wur frae wan o' the two places ah go tae," he declared — thereby revealing the totality of his contribution to society.

Ben Smith and the Consultant

Ben Smith was a distinguished, competent and much-admired Trade Union officer in the seventies and eighties. He was the Scottish regional Officer of NALGO - the Local Government Union. He was an Englishman who had taken readily to Scotland and the Scots.

He knew nothing about his antecedents. He had been a Barnardo's Boy and had no recollection of life prior to being with and of that wonderful organisation. He was clever, an attribute recognised by the senior staff at Barnardo's. As a result they channelled him to a good grammar school. On leaving school - and Barnardo's - at the age of 17 going on 18 he started work in a bank in the City.

By this time he had developed 'sympathetic leanings' towards the Soviet Union and the Communist Party. This in turn led to his taking up employment with a Russian bank. It was to lead to serious disenchantment. The more he saw of the Russian bank and its practices and procedures, the more he dealt with senior Russians, the more he learned of what was actually happening in the Soviet Union, the more disenchanted he became.

In one dramatic month he left the Communist Party and the bank and the hostel they provided. He turned to the Labour Party and to the world of the Unions. Being able, he rose quickly in the Union world while in both the Union and the Labour Party he emerged as the scourge of the Communist Party and its adulatory attitude towards the Soviet Union and its foreign policies.

We — that is, he and I — became firm friends. I was already friends with Norman Hogg, one of his immediate lieutenants, but Norman went into Parliament while I saw more and more of Ben. For example, we did weekend 'schools' together and for many years were Joint Tutors at the S.T.U.C. summer school. Another close friend of Ben's was James Milne, the General Secretary of the S.T.U.C. On first learning of and later witnessing this affinity, I was surprised — not least because Milne was a member of the Communist Party. But the more we saw of James Milne and the more we discussed a wide range of topics with him the more we perceived that his Communism was paper thin — tissue paper thin. Indeed, Ben believed that Jimmy would have left the Party had it not been for his wife Alice who was a firebrand and a real unquestioning member of the Communist Party. It was Ben's contention that had Jimmy resigned from the Party, Alice would have made his life intolerable.

Then Ben took ill and ended up in the Royal Infirmary in Glasgow with a urinary infection.

One evening one of his visitors was his son, an economist who taught at Strathclyde University. When he was leaving, the young man asked his dad if there was anything his father would like him to bring on his next visit.

Ben asked him to bring some sheets of graph paper, blue, red and green pens and a ruler.

Each Wednesday morning between ten and eleven o'clock a man wearing a white coat and an aura of authority swept into the ward and proceeded to walk through the ward at a fine rate of knots. As he did so, he was all bright and breezy. He called out comments and queries but never paused in either walking or pronouncement.

"How are we all today? Feeling better today, no doubt? Nurses — a grand set of young ladies. Everything fine?"

Here it was not at all clear whether these words were truly a question or a query. Ben chose to regard them as a question.

"Hello there," he cried and raced on, "can you spare a minute or two?"

The medic stopped and walked over to Ben's bed. He was clearly peeved that his flow had been checked.

"Did you want to see me?" he asked.

"Yes," said Ben. "You asked a question and I took it you wanted - or at least were not averse - to an answer. More particularly, would you mind looking at these graphs? May I take it that if these trend curves continue and the green line crosses and climbs away from the red and the red diminishes and disappears, then I can go home?"

The medic radiated surprise and modest delight.

"How ingenious," he commented. After a pause he continued. "Yes, if it is maintained, then you can go home at the weekend."

"Fine," said Ben, "will you please tell sister?"

"Yes," said the Medic, "yes, I shall."

Some years later the Chairman of the Greater Glasgow Health Trust retired and was succeeded by a friend. The man who retired was Jimmy Milne and the man who replaced him was Ben Smith.

He settled into this new job quickly and resolved not only to attend but to chair all Appointment Committees dealing with senior appointments.

A few months into his appointment such a Committee was called and amongst the contenders chosen for interview was the man of Ben's Royal Infirmary experience.

At some Appointment Committees, Ben confined himself to asking one question of all those to be interviewed. Ben's one recurring question was whether the applicant believed in ensuring that all his/her patients were informed on the state of play on their condition.

Given that Ben was consistent in his questioning, he found that applicants were equally consistent in contending that not only did they endorse that principle but that each of them argued he/she had always paid strict attention to honouring it.

That day, when it became time to reach a decision, the Committee was unanimous in deciding in favour of the doctor involved in the Royal Infirmary incident. Ben did not demur.

The medic was called back in and was offered the post. He accepted. Congratulations were offered, some folk clapped and others thumped the table.

Ben called for order. He went on to invite the new man to wait on for a spell. He in turn agreed.

Ben thanked the other candidates and they left.

When the door was closed and Ben and the medic were alone, Ben smiled at the about-to-be top Consultant.

"There are two points which I wish to raise with you," he observed.

"Certainly," beamed the man of success.

"The first is to say you rightly deserved this appointment. You were clearly the best qualified and the most suitable candidate. You have every right to be pleased."

"Thank you very much, Chairman."

"Not at all," said Ben. "Now for my second point: you are a liar!"

The successful candidate was very, very angry.

"Oh, no, Chairman, I am not prepared to sit here and be insulted and quite erroneously charged with matters of which I am innocent and ......"

Here Ben intervened.

"Hold on, hold your horses. Instead of being indignant, just look at these graphs."

And he slipped across the table the graphs of yesteryear.

Ben could see realisation dawning on the other's face.

"Oh, I see. I see what you mean."

"Good," said Ben. "Now go out and do your good work. And, this time, keep your patients informed."

The Young Footballer and the Manager

The Rangers Football Club of the war and immediate post-war years was very successful. Trophies were won regularly, bringing delight for their supporters and boredom and resignation on the part of others.

In the post-war years their defence was particularly competent and came to be known as 'The Iron Curtain'.

This was a shade unfair in that it did a dis-service to their forward line. All five forwards were very competent but the two outstanding players were Willie Waddell on the right wing and Willie Thornton in the middle. Waddell would cross the ball and, by head or by boot, Thornton would knock it beyond the opposition's goal-keeper into the back of the net.

Life has many twists. I never knew Willie Waddell, but I have come to know his brother, Walter, who is the most charming and gracious of men. Sadly, few folk would have said that of Willie.

Thornton I knew fleetingly. He was manager of Partick Thistle at a time when my assignment in the Ministry of Labour brought the Thistle ground in Firhill into my territory.

On one occasion he told me a story about the very early days of his career at Ibrox, with Rangers.

His story concerned the season 1938-39. He was 17 going on 18 and was a regular in the Rangers' reserve team which, in those days, was known as an 'A' team.

The young Thornton's team was in the players' dressing room on a Monday morning after the intensive training session. While the players were in various states of undress, the manager, a man called Struth, swept in. He walked on through and by the reserve players and others of lesser import and strode on to the top of the room where the older, experienced players like Meiklejohn and Dawson were fore-gathered. He engaged the group for some ten or twelve minutes of intense conversation.

On his way back out he stopped by our young hero.

"You, boy, what's your name, again?"

"Thornton, sir."

"Yes, Thornton. You scored twice for the A team on Saturday?"

"Yes, I did, sir."

"Well now, well done! Keep it up, lad," and with that he swept his way towards the door. He put his hand on the handle, but changed his mind and returned to Thornton.

"Tell me, Thornton, how much do we pay you?"

"A pound a week," was the reply.

Struth smiled. "A pound a week? Hmm, let's make that thirty shillings. Tell the accountant I said you are to get thirty shillings. I like a boy who cleans his shoes."

He left as the lad called out, "Thank you very much, Mr Struth."

Having told me his story, Thornton smiled.

"I hadn't the nerve to tell him that my mother brushed and polished my shoes every night."

Not Quite a Normal Night

Jean was an eager, clever, bright lass who lived in a modest home on the edge of the Glasgow conurbation. The household consisted of her parents, her wee brother and herself. At the time of this story she was ten years old and looking forward to her eleventh birthday.

One night, at the evening meal, her mother let her know that she wanted to speak to her and so, when the meal was over, she cleared the table and went on to help her mother with the washing and putting away the dishes. Later, when they were alone, her mother explained that her Aunty Betty was expecting a baby which was due shortly. Her uncle was working on the nightshift and she, the mother, did not want Betty to be alone: "So to prevent that, I want you to go over and stay the night with her. Come back in the morning for your breakfast and your school books." Jean complied readily with her mother's request.

Jean and her aunt Betty were to spend that night in an Anderson Shelter. That night was to be the first of the two nights of the Clydebank Blitz.

Next morning, after the 'all clear', while Jean and the aunt were having a gey modest breakfast, a boy called to say the uncle would not be home until the early afternoon as he had volunteered to help tidy up the factory which though it had escaped direct damage from the bombs, had experienced considerable secondary damage.

At half past eight Jean left the aunt's house and set out to walk home, see her mother, collect her brother and her books and go to school. She was a clever and intelligent child but when she turned the corner intending to cross to her own close, she stopped and stared in disbelief and then screamed.

Jean's close had gone and in its place there was a pile of rubble. Her close was gone; her mother and father had gone; her brother was gone; their modest possessions were gone, including her mother's fine dinner set of which she was so proud, as well as her father's favourite chair which had been a present from his wife for his fortieth birthday. Jean's 'good' dress for going to church on Sunday was gone, as was her brother's train set and his bag of marbles. Everything was gone! All she had in the world consisted of the clothes she was wearing.

But she was wrong. By the grace of God she had an uncle and aunt who hugged her, took her in and raised her.

She took her Higher Leaving Certificate and took a post in a city office. She met and married a young accountant who was also a part-time player for Rangers who played frequently in the first team with the financial rewards that went with that accomplishment. They had a very successful married life and she had and raised a family of her own.

But she never forgot — and never forgets — the first night of the Clydebank blitz.

There is a post-script to this story.

I volunteered for aircrew duties in the RAF and expressed a preference for Bomber Command. It so happened I never finished the training; we were told we were "surplus to requirements". Yet I had friends who served on Lancasters, Halifaxes and Stirlings. Most of them were killed. Bomber Command, where every man was a volunteer, had the heaviest casualties per thousand men of any service. Notwithstanding this sacrifice, there was no campaign ribbon for Bomber Command. It appears that the Government was embarrassed by the loss of life in the allied bombings of Dresden, Hamburg and Berlin.

In the late winter or early spring of 1941 the people of Clydebank and many other British cities would have gladly acclaimed the men of Bomber Command.

The Last Full Day of the Holidays

Grace Johnston was one of our colleagues in the Ministry of Labour. She was a good colleague and despite the pressures of the job was invariably of equable temperament.

One of the stories she related referred to their annual holidays when she and her brothers were all of school age

Traditionally they and their mother, who was a widow, had two weeks every July. They invariably went to Millport, every year to the same house. Traditionally, Millport, the only town on the Great Cumbrae island off the north Ayrshire coast, was deemed a very safe place for a family holiday. One reason was that then there was very little road traffic. Now car-ferries run frequently from Largs on the mainland to the slipway on the north-east side of the island. Notwithstanding the marked increase in the number of vehicles, something of the old tradition lingers on and the hiring of bicycles looms large in the holiday programme of most young people.

The Johnston children had all hired bikes and for the last full day their mother hired a bicycle and joined them on a quasi-ceremonial circuit of the island with one picnic at Fintry Bay on the west coast and a second stop at Fairhaven on the east coast.

Such was the Johnston Convention.

Then came the dramatic summer.

Mrs Johnston prided herself on being a good organiser. Certainly she was methodical, maybe rigorously so. Each Christmas she ensured that one of the children, usually the youngest, gave her a new diary as a Christmas present. Being both Scottish and superstitious, a not unusual blend, she did not write in it until the New Year arrived. Her first entries were to plot the fortnight in July when they would be in Millport and then to mark in St Valentine's

Day to contact Mrs Caggie, the lady in Riddrie who owned the wee house in Millport. Firstly, she would ascertain its availability and then politely negotiate the price for having it for their fortnight.

This year proved to be different. Dreadful news came. Mrs Caggie said she had sold the house to a Riddrie neighbour, a Mrs Abercrombie, but there was no point in phoning her. Both Mr and Mrs Abercrombie came from big families and she had made it clear a plethora of relatives would be occupying the house in Millport from Easter week through to the September weekend, as the Glasgow Bank holiday was known.

The phone conversation with Mrs Caggie ended on a further dull note. Mrs Caggie did not know of anyone with a house in Millport who "let it out" over the summer.

That evening gloom and despondency hovered over the Johnston kitchen table.

What could they do?

No one had an answer.

Some nights later the mother came in from the Kirk Guild in a state of some elation. Over the inevitable 'cup of tea' a friend called McMaster had told her about her neighbour, a Mrs McKirdy, who had a rather fine holiday house which she let out but not in August. There were two known disadvantages. The first was that it was said to be a shade 'pricey'. The second was that, given the hopes and aspirations of the Johnston family, the McKirdy house — fine though the house might be — was on Arran, in Lamlash to be precise.

Nevertheless, Mrs Johnston phoned Mrs McKirdy and wrapped the respectability and acceptability of Mrs McMaster round herself and her offspring.

Yes, the house was for occasional let.

Yes, she readily accepted that a friend of Mrs McMaster would be a suitable temporary tenant.

The house was available for 'their' fortnight in July though it would have to be left in spanking condition as the next occupant would be her sister-in-law, Mr McKirdy's sister.

Mrs Johnston pledged it would be left in pristine condition.

"Good," said Mrs McKirdy. "Now as to price, it would be ......" and here she quoted a price double that which the Johnstons paid Mrs Craggie for the Millport house.

Mrs Johnston gulped and said she would take it.

Mrs McKirdy said the keys would be given, come the time, to Mrs McMaster and could be returned by the same route.

When she reported to Grace and her brothers, one of the lads, the eldest, snorted and complained about the price but added: "Arran gets the rugby types. They would be glad to pay more as a means of keeping the football types away from their watering hole."

And so that summer instead of Largs, the car ferry to the slipway and the bus to Millport, they took the train to Ardrossan, the big car ferry to Arran and a taxi to the McKirdy house in Lamlash.

Their Arran expedition had begun, bikes were hired and Whiting Bay and Brodick fully explored. As the last full day approached the question arose: would Mrs Johnston hire a bike and join them in cycling round the island?

The oldest boy said he had consulted a map and the road followed the coast all the way. He observed that fortunately the corner of the island had been 'clipped off'.

He pronounced that they should all go and have the first picnic at Blackwaterfoot and the second at the other end of the island.

On the day in question they sallied forth in a southerly direction. The going was easy, with the sea on their left. Both picnics went well. But within minutes of leaving Lochranza, they found that the road climbed as it made its way through, to them, massive mountains on its way to the east coast village of Corrie.

By the time they reach Brodick their timetable was in ruins. They had failed to allow for the size of Arran and the number of mountains in the northern half.

When they got home to Lamlash their mother was exhausted. Grace had to help her mother into her night clothes. Meanwhile the boys had to pack the wicker hamper and tie it up with rope as well as locking the padlock. The second son was in the scouts and specialised in knots and allied matters. He not only supervised the roping of the hamper but prepared loops like handles near each corner.

On the following day, the day of their return to Glasgow and their home in Bellahouston, Grace, who was returning to enter the sixth and last year of her secondary education, ordered and paid for the taxi to Brodick pier. There are diverse accounts as to how they got from the main road to the gangplank leading to the boat which was to take them to Ardrossan and the Glasgow train.

Some claim that they saw the four children carrying the hamper while a still exhausted mother sat on the hamper and was occasionally saved from falling by Grace's deft use of her free hand.

The overall outcome of the Arran adventure was that from Hallowe'en onwards they searched and enquired after a house in Millport.

Their assessment of the deviation was given by Grace. On her first day back at school her friend Edith Swann asked:

"How was Lamlash?"

Grace looked thoughtful.

"Alright," she said, "but it was not Millport!"

The Northern Manager

This is a story which purports to be about football but, truth to tell, there is gey little football in it. I obtained it from my friend, the late Robert Crampsey. But before I relate it I would inject a theory of my own. I have long contended that there is a strong relationship between the success of a club and the economic prosperity of the town of the club and its environs. I argue that the success of East Fife in the immediate post-war years was to a large extent due to the prosperity, at that time, of the mining industry in that part of the Kingdom. So, too, the success of Aberdeen at and around the time of their success in defeating Real Madrid was attributable not only to the skill and competence of the players and the near-genius of Alex Ferguson the manager, but also to the prosperity and impressive income flow pouring into the city from the North Sea oil industry. By the same token, as I see it, the success of the clubs in the north of England in the late forties, the fifties and the early sixties was in no small part due to the continuing prosperity emanating from full employment and high wages squeezed out of employers by well-organised and occasionally bloody-minded trade unions.

Part of my argument, then, is that it is most significant that the dramatic 'Stanley Matthews cup-final' was between two northern clubs – Blackpool and Bolton Wanderers. True, Blackpool was no grimy mill town but it benefited from the then prosperity of the places which were.

All that said, we can now turn to the Robert Crampsey story. The setting is the middle fifties and the principal character is a man in his late fifties or early sixties who is the manager of a football club in the North of England. In the recent past they have been doing well in that for three seasons they ended fairly high in the First

Division and in two other seasons they had experienced exciting and impressive runs in the F.A. cup.

Quite apart from their performances, the manager is popular and held in high regard. As one of his intelligent players put it: "He is of a congenial demeanour and has a friendly disposition."

There is, however, one serious deficiency: he knows nothing about football. He looks after his players. He can and does give great advice to them all on such matters as where to buy a car and where to go on holiday, on where to live and how to obtain a mortgage at a reasonable cost. He will even give advice on their girlfriends, steering them toward some young ladies and away from others.

On football matters he was well nigh silent. On both strategy and tactics he had nothing to say. As they were ready to run onto the park, all he could do was to wish them good luck.

But in the season of our story they were not doing well, indeed they were hovering just above the relegation zone.

This situation was substantially attributable to a softness and lack of action on the part of the manager. It was well recognised that he should have moved some players on to other clubs. Some supporters thought that he should have moved on most of his older players because many of them had lost their pace or zeal or both. In short, the club needed fresh blood. It had some young players but did not have enough of them.

On the last day of the season the team and the officials found themselves on a train. They were due to change at Crewe and continue to South Wales where they were to play a most difficult and important game. In the event of their winning all would be well, whereas were they to draw, things would probably be fine. If they lost, however, they would be in very real danger of relegation though that in turn would depend on results elsewhere.

As the train rattled along the two full-backs started a conversation. The young and somewhat jejune left back observed that the match that awaited them was so vital, so important, that the manager would be compelled to talk football and not merely give them advice but actually tell them in specific terms what they had to do. The young lad was so enthused, so taken up by his own assertion that he went on to contend that the manager would tell each and every player what he had to do.

The right-back, a much older man, who should have been released a couple of seasons earlier, scoffed at his young colleague's contention.

"You are wrong," he said and went on: "The boss is a decent enough bloke, but he won't do what you suggest because he can't do what you have in mind. It is all beyond him. He will not tell us what to do because he has no understanding of the game. He is a good manager in that he has a good hold on the business affairs of the club but that does not make him a good football manager. In short, you are wrong!"

"Bet you," said the lad. "I'll bet you a pound he talks tactics today."

"You are on," said his fellow defender. "A pound it is, payable on the journey back."

The kick-off was scheduled for three o'clock and precisely on two-thirty the manager came into the dressing room – a thing he had never done before. He looked stern and glowered at everyone in the room. "Now then," he opened, "at ten minutes to three I want everyone out 'cept the team. At ten to three I want all the rest of you out..... all you so-called journalists, all you hangers-on.... Come ten to three, all you lot — out!"

Having made his declaration he turned and left whereupon the young left-back grinned at the old right back.

"Told you," he said.

"We'll see," said the other.

At two-fifty precisely the manager returned. He held the door wide open.

"Right then, you heard me last time. All you chancers, out.... out now. On you go, out."

When they had gone, he closed the door and stood with his back against it thereby denying any potential intruders. He looked stern.

"Right then," he opened. "Right now, pay attention, every one of you for this is important. When final whistle goes, up tunnel and into the bath. No muckin' about chatting. Train goes at 5.18 and we don't want to miss it."

They got their draw, and the old right-back got his pound.

The I. T. Campaign of 1982

As I recall it, it was Lord Allanbrooke who observed that during his Premiership in the years of the Second World War, Winston Churchill had ten of what he regarded as good ideas to win the war. But Allanbrooke went on to say that for every ten, nine would have lost the war and one won it. His difficulty and that of his immediate colleagues was to identify the one good idea and hold a feasibility exercise on it while meantime jettisoning the other nine.

In 1981 Margaret Thatcher in the course of her Premiership proposed nominating the following year of 1982 for an Awareness Campaign in which to invite the attention of the public to the great advantages of Information Technology. As I recall it, the Government was not unco' keen on spending the money on the scheme. There was a preparedness to inject some lubricating money – but not much! In addition, I remember in the course of the year of the campaign having been taken aside to be told that the real innovator of the plan was the appropriate minister while yet others argued that it was all due to Sir Cyril Taylor who was a friend of and confidant of the then Mrs Thatcher.

All of this and more was the background to a meeting in Glasgow in late '81 of a motley collection of I.T. experts who regarded themselves as volunteer samurai and at the same time, in their collective role, as the embryonic Scottish Committee for the Campaign. They were not alone in this dual capacity. As though by spontaneous combustion similar embryonic committees were emerging throughout the U.K.

Most of the guys – and they were nearly exclusively male – knew or knew of their potential colleagues. By and large they recognised one another's competence. Some were more enthusiastic than others and were looking forward to the implementation of the campaign's events. Others were there out of a sense of duty while yet others were there because their employers had nominated them and had told them to attend.

I was not in attendance at that meeting but I inferred later that their discussion was learned and imaginative but almost devoid of structure. The longer they went on the more they realised that they needed a Chairman and that no-one present was keen to take on the task. I was told later that a member of my staff was there and was asked whether the University could provide a potential Chairman. She observed that her boss was an experienced Chairman though his knowledge of I.T. was thin. To a man they acclaimed this as a well-nigh perfect solution, not least as the likelihood was that he would be neutral and would not be predisposed to favour any I.T. company over another.

So it was that I emerged as the Chairman of and the least informed and least competent member of the Scottish Committee of the 1982 I.T. Campaign.

It proved to be a full and demanding year. We were all in full-time employment and had to be available for both meetings and events as and when we could from already heavily committed diaries. My biggest problem was in obtaining sufficient funds to cover travel cost, postage and the like. So far as accommodation was concerned, the Scottish Development Agency in Bothwell Street Glasgow gave us two rooms but unfortunately they were at opposite ends of the same corridor. In addition, my own University let us have free use of some large lecture theatres though that in turn meant that some events had to be held at times when the lecture rooms were free rather than the ideal times for our potential audiences.

Obtaining a modest supply of support staff proved difficult. I remembered that there was a Government scheme whereby a socially commendable organisation could have the services of an unemployed graduate. We applied and were duly granted a bright and willing young man, whereupon we ran into a bureaucratic nightmare as to who would be his nominal employer. We were not allowed to employ anyone: it had been assumed that such staff as we could muster would be 'seconded' from I.T. firms.

So far as our young graduate was concerned, the Scottish Development Agency was not averse to receiving his salary from the Job Creation scheme and paying his salary, after due deductions, into his current account, but as I remember it that ran into difficulties as the appropriate trade union objected to the Agency paying someone it did not employ. I cracked that one by threatening to write to all the broadsheets exposing the impasse and to hold a press conference inviting attention to our frustration.

My colleagues and I were all in full-time employment. We had then to squeeze time for both meetings and events into our diaries.

We stuck at it throughout the year. Doggedly and tenaciously we offered and held 287 events throughout the length and breadth of Scotland. Some were very successful, some were disappointing, a few were failures. The successful varied considerably in scale – from a lecture in a library in the Vale of Leven with an attendance of seven to a presentation on 'The Office of Tomorrow and the Day after Tomorrow'. This topic attracted audiences, mainly of school pupils in the senior forms and generally, of between 500 and 800 to each presentation. After its three appearances in Glasgow it went on tour round our major cities.

One very successful event was a hands-on demonstration of spreadsheets by a Depute Head of an Edinburgh College. This was very well received, so much so he was asked to repeat it again and again. It ended with him doing it six times in the course of the year. One man phoned to say he had implemented spreadsheets in his business and had been rewarded with a marked increase in the efficiency of his Accounts Section.

Then again, we had a leading Scottish author who requested a private demonstration of Word Processing. She was so taken with what she saw she immediately set about acquiring such equipment and later reported that as a result she had trebled her output with the consequential knock-on benefit to the Scottish economy.

On one memorable day of atrocious wintry weather we were doing one of the presentations on 'The Office of the Future' when a formidable lady swept up to me.

"I understand you are in charge here," she declared. "We are…"— and here she gave me the name of a very good Lanarkshire school

— and continued: "We should be 42 but are here with a mere 25. Dysentery and diarrhoea in the school! Where are the toilets?"

When the year was over it transpired that the Scottish effort had been the most successful in the whole of the U.K. The second best had been the Northern Ireland Committee led by a very fine young man called Bob McLaughlin.

The 1982 I.T. Campaign was officially closed by Mrs Thatcher at an event in the Barbican in London. She was in grand form and as I recall it used the transparent glass auto-cues for the first time. She told us all, including some of the English Regional Committees which had been rather pathetic, that we had all done extremely well, whereupon she announced that there was to be a follow-up campaign which was to run for three years from 1983 until 1985. On hearing this most of my colleagues applauded loudly but let me know privately that they had had enough and were going back to what they had been doing in 1981.

The 83-85 campaign did some good work but it did not have the buzz and excitement and intensity of the 1982 exercise.

Such was the story of the exhausting and some ways the amazing story of the year of the great I.T. Awareness Campaign.

There was as I saw it one unexpected incident. To my recollection, it was that year's Moderator of the General Assembly of the Kirk who invited my attention to Alvin Toffler's book 'Future Shock' in which he discussed the rapid rate of technological change in the nineteenth and twentieth centuries and then went on to contend that such change, which we were inclined to regard as dramatic, would be seen as almost standing still when compared with the rate of change which was about to hit us. The vindication of that contention is all too apparent when we consider the changes and the new equipment we have adopted in the thirty or so years since 1982.

The inference of the point just made is that this game will never finish and that yet more change will be introduced at a faster and faster rate.

There is one point which should perhaps have been made much, much earlier and which arose at the beginning of our Awareness Campaign. The formal opening or launching of the Scottish

Campaign took place in the Staff Club of the University of Edinburgh on the eighteenth of January. The platform consisted of three of us: the Minister of State at the Scottish Office, Mr Alex Fletcher; a Deputy Chairman of our Committee, Mrs Christine Davis who went on to be the Chairman of the Scottish Legal Aid Board and later still of Energy Action Scotland; and myself.

All three of us spoke but in my remarks I nearly killed the Minister. I argued that Information Technology in the U.K. was like culture in the Soviet Union in that in the Soviet Union culture was what the Minister of Culture said was culture while here Information Technology was what the appropriate Minister said was Information Technology.

Christine told me that at my reference to the Soviet Union, Mr Fletcher turned grey. He did not die then, but did die a few years later. He was a fine Minister and a fine man. I did wonder whether he ever forgave me for my casting aspersions on the rôle of the Minister in regard to Information Technology.

Rose

This story is being written in the delightful town of Puerto Pollensa in the north of Majorca in the Balearic Islands in the Mediterranean Sea.

That is very appropriate for it was in Puerto Pollensa that I had the pleasure and privilege of meeting and getting to know Rose. I have to admit, though, that I would not be writing about her had it not been for an incident in the Commons in the closing months of the Brown Government.

During Prime Minister's Questions one day Brown was at the Despatch Box. He was scoffing at a Tory question which had gone beyond questioning to allude to, indeed advocate, a different policy.

Brown was for none of it and in the course of his reply alluded to "policies conjured up on the playing fields of Eton". I would have thought that such a sweeping observation was standard stuff for the knock-about which 'Prime Minister's Questions' has become. On this occasion, however, it seemed to have struck some raw nerve: maybe the retort was indicative of how many Old Etonians decorate the Tory benches.

Anyway, the remark from Brown signalled an uproar which surprised Brown, many of his supporters and me, listening to it on Radio 4.

The drift of the Tory riposte was not as accurately and succinctly expressed as the Classics and English masters at Eton would have wished. It was two-fold.

Firstly, they regarded this as a Labour revival of what they saw as 'the old and discredited class-war system' which was both wrong and unbecoming.

Secondly, they argued that it is perfectly possible for a man to be someone of substance, to be well-off and yet be a man of compassion for his less affluent neighbours.

I recall rather well my own response to these contentions. I remember commenting aloud that however well-intentioned such folk might be, however sincere their sympathy for the poor and deprived might seem, they have no real understanding of the horrors of abject poverty.

Later that day I told my wife about what I had heard and how I had reacted to it. My wife nodded and in turn recalled an incident in the thirties when she was a child and not long at school. A male neighbour had died and on the evening of the day of his funeral her mother had invited the widow in for 'a wee cup of tea' which turned out to be a knife and fork meal. The new widow was most appreciative of the quiet hospitality. When she was leaving she put her hand in a pocket in her 'pinny' and withdrew her purse which she opened. She showed that it contained fourpence. "That," she observed, "is my total wealth in the world," and then she returned to her own flat/house, call it what you will.

And so to Rose.

In their day Rose and her husband had been the jitter-bugging champions of Greenock and Port Glasgow. Life for her and her husband and their four children was fairly hard but they found it pleasant and reasonably satisfactory.

Then it all changed: it all went wrong.

Rose's husband died.

Rose realised she had to obtain work but found that a full-time job from 9 till 5 or from 8 to 4.45 was almost impossible to obtain. But Rose was resilient. She found not one job but a series, a 'collection' of diverse wee jobs.

These jobs obliged her to rise shortly after five in the morning and from six to nearly seven she worked in a local newsagent's shop sorting out the newspapers for the corps of delivery boys who arrived at 7.30 to take them on their rounds. By the time the boys arrived at the shop, Rose was away and had started her first stint of the day as a school cleaner, working until 8.30 when she raced home to make sure the children were up and washed and dressed and had had their breakfast.

At 8.45 a.m. she saw them off to school, gave herself a late, frugal breakfast and left for a grocer's shop where she stacked cans and packages until after 11 o'clock when she went home to see to washing and ironing and dusting and other household chores. After twelve her children came home for soup and sandwiches and after 1 o'clock they all left while their mother went to a supermarket to stack more shelves. By four o'clock the children were returning from their school while their mother made for 'her' school for her second stint as a cleaner.

By six in the evening they were all home for the main meal of the day, and by 7.30 pm the dishes had been washed and put away. Rose saw them settled to their homework and told them what they could watch on the television whereupon she left to go to a nearby golf club where she collected and washed glasses and occasionally served drinks till after 10 p.m. It was often after 11 p.m. when she returned home, made herself a late cup of tea, said her prayers and washed and got to bed before midnight struck.

When I met Rose she was 72 and, in the Glasgow idiom, 'smoked like a lum'.

Her children became a great credit to her. The one I knew best was, by 2008, a senior administrator in a Scottish university.

Rose died in 2010. Her proud boast was that she had missed Sunday Mass only twice in her entire life.

Cameron and Osborne and the other 19 millionaires in the Conservative-Liberal Cabinet claim, no doubt sincerely, that they respond to and in a way admire folk like Rose. But there is a void.

Though Rose and the senior ministers were citizens, more precisely subjects, of the one State, they lived in different worlds.

One of the difficulties of Cameron and most of his Cabinet is that they know not the pain and strain of real poverty. In one sense this is not their fault – but they could acknowledge that they know nothing about it.

"Magrit"

The background to this story is a remarkable economic phenomenon which, in Britain alone, involves millions of households and sees millions upon millions of pounds being handed over every week. Yet the financial aspect of this economic activity is seldom raised in conversation, which in one sense is surprising because it is illegal in two regards. Firstly, in extremely few cases is there any assessment for Income Tax and, secondly, it would seem that there is virtually no payment of National Insurance Contributions – either class one by the employer(s) or class two by those who do the work. It is part of the black economy. In my experience professional economists never refer to it, notwithstanding its scale, the fact that it is an enormous transfer of income and that were it to cease leafy suburbia would not prevail as it does.

The operatives in this massive activity are the army of women who sally forth from their homes, some of them every day, to clean, tidy, make more presentable, the homes of others.

In Glasgow and the West of Scotland they are called 'cleaners'. In parts of London each is known as 'the lady who does', whilst in the prosperous parts of Northern Ireland they are called 'treasures' or 'little treasures'.

The ladies who do the work nearly all live in working-class areas, substantially, but by no means exclusively, in what were built as Local Authority Housing Estates.

Those who draw on such services are mainly but by no means exclusively female. There seems to be an accepted policy of not using the word 'employ', other words, including euphemisms, being preferred.

Those who use such services tend to fall into three distinguishable groups.

First, the elderly and those disabled by such ailments as arthritis and sciatica. The second group are the professionals and others relatively well paid – the academics, those in medicine, the law and the money and financial services market and yet other groups such as musicians, actors and airline employees. The third group consists of affluent or relatively affluent ladies who prefer to shop, play bridge or golf or do 'good works' rather than doing the 'hoovering' and the ironing.

Our story arises from this world. Mrs Buckley and her daughter lived in a six-apartment bungalow in the south-side of Glasgow. For years they had been blessed by recourse to the facilities of Anne Marie, an industrious and intelligent (the qualities do not always run in harness) treasure. Anne Marie had been a widow with three children of school age. Then disaster struck. Anne Marie went on a parish pilgrimage and met and in time married Michael, a widower.

The Buckley ladies were pleased for Anne Marie and even for Michael but they were plunged into a lengthy period of having no cleaner. Friends were quizzed, phone calls were made, the daughter tried email enquiries. They prayed and their prayers were answered though God did not provide a second Anne Marie. God, in his infinite wisdom, provided Magrit.

Magrit had of course been baptised Margaret but that name was unduly long for her mother, for the rest of her family, and, consequently, for Margaret herself.

When the Buckley ladies interviewed Margaret/Magrit they were appalled in that she was a tough cookie who was not slow in spelling out what she would do and not do.

"Ah scrub ra flair," she observed. "Ah don't like mopping. It's no right somehow. Ah dae ra hooverin', wash dishes if needed, pit ra clothes in ra washin' machine, take oot ra claes, hang 'em up and iron them. But youse should know ah don't dae brasses. Ah don't like brasses, so ah don't. Oh, an' anither thing: ah like a Kit-Kat biscuit wae ma mug o' tea. It's no' that ah really want tea but ah dae need a lavvy break."

When the 'interview' was over, the Buckley ladies looked at each other. Neither spoke nor was there any nodding or other body language. Yet each sensed that, despite dreadful reservations and misgivings, they had to accept Magrit. There was little choice: it was Magrit or nothing.

Acceptance offered and agreed, it was arranged that Magrit would come on Tuesdays and Thursdays from 10 a.m. until 12.30 p.m. The rate would be the 'going rate' in the district.

When Magrit arrived on her first day of work, she rang the bell very loudly.

When Mrs Buckley opened the door, Magrit bounced in before being invited so to do. Never slow, she asked:

"Hello, hen. Feelin' oany bettah?" Yet to her credit, within two minutes her coat was off and the electric carpet sweeper was out and was purring away.

One evening some five or six months after Magrit's engagement Mrs Buckley confided in her daughter. She revealed she had steeled herself to ask Magrit to pull out the beds and 'hoover' below them.

The next day, she voiced her request. Magrit looked perplexed.

"Aye, aw right, if that's whit you want," she replied, but raced on. "Whit fur ur we daen' that fur? Hive youse drapped something, like?"

What a wonderful world we live in. I have heard that a recurring question arising at coffee mornings is: "What kind of car does your cleaner drive?"

The Facility for Language

For the life of me I cannot recall the year in which I heard the programme, though I would guess it was some fifteen or eighteen years back. It was one of a series of programmes broadcast on BBC Radio 4 on the English Language, this one with a not insubstantial input from Frank Delaney. The particular episode was based on Dublin and argued that the Irish have a great facility for language.

As I recall it, three Professors of Language and/or Linguistics were interviewed. It led to a good discussion and it did not take long for them and the interviewer to agree that the Irish do have a facility for language. Then again, it is most pronounced in the West of Ireland, and, within the West, at its most pronounced in the 'Gaeltacht' areas, where, so the plan ran, only Irish would be spoken though tourism and the penetration of the BBC in both radio and television gave that bit of social engineering a very severe knock.

One participant was most enthused – and adamant. He went on to contend that if you want to bring out the best of it you had to speak not in customised English but in English versions of Irish language phraseology.

As an example of what he had in mind, he urged his listeners who encountered people, particularly elderly people, from the West of Ireland NOT to say "How do you do?" or "How are you?" These were English questions not just in the language but in phraseology. What he urged his listeners to do was to ask "What way with you?" and to slip in the Christian name of the person to whom the query is addressed. Thereupon he gave three examples.

"What way with you, Liam?"

"I am struggling along between the two great enormities of life."

"And what would they be, Liam?"

"Birth and Death."

"What way with you, Eithne?"

"God Almighty, if I felt a bit better I would go to the doctor."

"What way with you, Padraig?

"I am like a chipped vase on the top shelf of the dresser: I have me good face to the world."

Sometimes I come across, here in Britain, people from the West of Ireland. One such is a priest, now quite elderly, who has spent some thirty or forty years in Liverpool.

When he is asked how he is, he invariably smiles and says:

"Better than I deserve to be, thanks be to God."

Collectively the Irish are a treasure trove of colourful language – and wisdom.

Condignation

This story goes back to the middle eighties. I heard it from an academic colleague, Professor Tom Markus, an architect. We had been at an Energy Conference at Aviemore. For quite different, disparate reasons we had to leave early and so it was we travelled together on a train back to Glasgow.

Tom told me that when he joined the University the 'new' School of Architecture was being built and the department had no room for him. It was then that the Maths Department came up trumps. They found a room for him – a small room but it was his. It was to be a temporary arrangement. When the new Architecture Building was ready for occupancy he would join his professional colleagues there.

One day in the waiting period Tom Markus was joined for lunch in the staff club by Peter Paulson, a professor of Chemistry. The chat was good but their table was needed for other potential diners so they agreed to withdraw to Tom's temporary abode for coffee.

While they were again deep in conversation over the Markus-made coffee they became conscious of groaning noises and heavy breathing. Neither spoke but each looked at the other. Perplexity reigned. Thereupon the door opened and a head peered round the door and into the room and gave voice to a protracted 'Ah'. The visitor was Joe Gradowski, a former Polish soldier who had married a Glasgow lady, a sister of Janet Buchan. Joe was then the Senior Technician in the Architecture Department.

Joe apologised for the intrusion but raced on to explain that 'they' had decided to bring the departmental meeting forward, from 2.30 to 2 o'clock. They were anxious that Professor Markus should know about this change: they did not want him arriving at 2.30 and, perhaps, thinking they had deliberately not informed him and had rushed through some matter of which he would have disapproved. Joe continued to race on, this time to say they could not phone him as the electricity was down. Then again the lifts were off as well – for the same reason.

Tom Markus felt obliged yet embarrassed. He knew that Joe Gradowski had recently had a serious heart operation. He had returned to work at the beginning of the week and was supposed to be working half-time.

Tom Markus looked at Joe and thanked him and went on to say ".......and I am doubly grateful in that you climbed all those stairs and you in your condition."

Joe protested. He argued that it had not been too bad; he observed that he had managed "just fine" – though his earlier groaning and heavy breathing belied him. "Anyway," he concluded, "it was only the fourth condignation."

The two professors spoke at once: what did he mean by 'condignation'? Speaking simultaneously they, duly, observed they were on level four, or on the fourth floor or even on the fourth storey. Why, they wanted to know, had Joe not used one of these terms? What gave with this 'condignation' caper?

Joe looked embarrassed and stumbled his way through his explanation. He did know level, storey and floor but had been temporarily confused. He knew the Polish word which was 'condignatio' and he had found over the years that if a Polish word finished with an O and one added an N, it frequently gave one the English word.

The professors smiled their understanding and that was that but it was not over. There were two other matters.

The first was that thereafter the two professors kept teasing Joe. When either of them met Joe they would greet him and ask: "What 'condignation' are you on today, Joe?" They overdid it and not unnaturally Joe was rather peeved.

Eventually, notwithstanding the difference in ranking, Joe told them — in the style of a sergeant-major addressing a major — that they had had their laughs at his expense. He would be grateful, he asserted, were they to drop it.

Nothing happened for some months until one evening in high summer Tom Markus was working in his garden when his wife came out to tell him that Peter Paulson was on the phone and wanted to speak to him. When they conversed Paulson told him that another Chemistry professor had gone to America for a swop year. He and the American with whom he was 'swopping' were living in each other's house. Before going to the States the Brit had bought all ten volumes of the full Oxford University Dictionary. But as the American had some very young children he had entrusted his acquisition to Peter Paulson for safe-keeping. Paulson explained to Tom Markus that he had just looked up 'condignation' and there it was.

"Condignation: floor, level, storey of a building. Last known use in written English —1643."

Joe Gradowski deserved an apology! Tom Markus agreed.

That, then, is the 'Condignation' story as told to me by Professor Markus on the train from Aviemore to Glasgow. For years I have told it to friends and occasionally checked some aspects of it with Tom Markus.

Yet something held me back from writing this tale. I knew what caused the hesitation. I wanted further confirmation of the existence of 'condignation'.

My wife and I bought the two-volume Shorter Oxford Dictionary – but it was not there. I found that a friend had the multi-volume version, and he reported that he could not find it. This merely fortified my hesitancy.

Then quite recently I was at a church coffee morning and a Deacon – Deacon John Cairns – to whom I had told the story, reported that he had looked up 'condignation' on the internet and voilà, the Lord be praised, there it was.

The piece deals with the conversion of a hotel into a sort of spa or health resort in Eastern Europe. We are told that one 'condignation' has been set aside for designated treatments.

Both Peter Paulson and Joe Gradowski are now dead. 'Condignation' lives on – just!

Uncle Jim's Wee Team

My mother was a Morrison, Jean Morrison. She was one of the seven children born to James and Annie Morrison who both came from small-holdings on gey marginal land outside Portadown. They came to Scotland in the eighties of the Nineteenth Century and never returned. The other six children consisted of three boys and three girls. The oldest boy, for that matter the oldest child, was called John after his grandfather back in Ireland. As a young man John was fortunate in that he inherited a hairdresser's business from his Uncle Patrick, a bachelor brother of his mother. Truth to tell, it was a run-of-the-mill barber's shop but John had the foresight to introduce a Ladies facility, no bigger than the square-footage of two telephone kiosks, in which in the twenties and thirties he provided so-called permanent waving for his female patrons. John was a very strong and competent swimmer. He spent most of his free time running not one but two amateur swimming clubs, both operating out of the Gorbals public baths.

The more successful and consequently better-known of the two clubs was the Southside Amateurs and his own two sons and younger daughter were proficient and prominent members of the club with the result that the many display cabinets in his house groaned with the weight of the many trophies which they all had won.

The youngest brother, Thomas, died at the age of ten. His nightgown caught fire and he died of his burns. This sort of tragedy was commonplace a century ago and it was not until after the Second World War that such incidents became extremely rare.

This story, however, concerns the middle brother James, known within the family as Jim. There was a certain mild flamboyance about him, a situation reflected in his somewhat chequered career.

On leaving school he was a sales assistant in a gents' outfitters but in the early months of the Great War he volunteered for the Army and with a silver tongue and a brass neck working in harness talked himself into a commission in an Irish regiment. He proved to be very fortunate in that he was never sent to the Western front where the casualty rates for young lieutenants was as high as that for rear-gunners in Bomber Command in the Second World War. After a spell at Cobh near Cork he and the rest of the battalion were sent to Thessalonika in Greece. From there he was involved in some minor action in the Eastern Mediterranean.

On his release from the Army he opened a shop specialising in hats and caps for gentlemen. This precarious venture staggered through the Twenties but was blown away by the Great Depression of the early thirties.

From the closure of the shop to the middle thirties Jim went through a very difficult time. As often as not, he was unemployed and claiming Unemployment Benefit but an alert supervisor had spotted that Jim had a facility for numbers with the result that from time to time he was invited to the other side of the counter. These episodes never lasted long and he had to return to the public side of the counter. His fortune turned in the middle of the decade when he happened to be working in his local Employment Exchange and was given the opportunity to sit an examination. He passed and as a result he found himself appointed as a Clerical Officer in the Ministry of Labour. This was a God-send: he was an established Civil Servant.

Jim was a very generous man, generous with his time and generous with his money – when he had any to spare. From the time I was five years of age until I was eight or nine he would come most Saturdays about two in the afternoon and we would go out on some expedition. Sometimes he would take me to a cinema, usually the Bedford in Eglinton St., sometimes we would go to a football match and here we had the choice of four nearby grounds – Hampden for Queen's Park, Cathkin for Third Lanark, Shawfield the home ground of Clyde or Parkhead for the formidable Celtic.

In addition there were Saturdays when we just went into town to Woolworths and the big Department Stores with magnificent Toy Departments. On such occasions we would almost always finish in

Woolworths where he would buy me a toy soldier which generally cost tuppence. Later when I was older I could see that the shopping days were more frequent during his spells of being out of work, the two pennies and the walk into and home from town being cheaper than either the football match or two seats in the cinema.

Later still I came to realise that he was a formidable card player. He did not play poker but he was a very good bridge player – no doubt a throw-back to his days in the Officers' Mess. By the same token he was a successful player at whist and ladies were always glad to partner him at Whist Drives.

Jim was a bachelor: he never married. About the time when I was starting school there was a courtship of sorts with a most unsuitable lady who was a peroxide blonde. My three aunts, I learned later, had denounced her as a gold-digger. There was no gold but when his business faltered so too did the romance.

Like most men of the period he was a heavy smoker and worked his way through about eighty cigarettes a day.

Neither of the two uncles I came to know was an avid reader of books whereas my three aunts, my mother and their mother invariably had a book on the go and occasionally had two or three overlapping throughout the week.

Yet Jim devoured newspapers though I came to suspect he read only the Sports pages and that even there he did not stray far beyond the pages devoted to football.

On a Saturday in his spells of modest affluence, he surpassed himself by buying 21 newspapers – all Sports editions of the three Glasgow papers, the *Times*, the *News* and the *Citizen*. This phenomenon started with the three mid-day Sports editions progressing through two editions with half-time scores and a plurality of editions with final results until about seven o'clock when he would buy the three copies of the Final Sports Edition which not only provided the avid reader with the results of all senior games played in the United Kingdom but the results of all Junior Football games and the same for Rugby matches played in Scotland and narrative reports on all the more important matches. Those three Final editions and a chair by the fire-side saw him through to bed-time.

During the week he would go out to play cards in some club or wherever but on Saturdays during the football season it was the papers and the fire that saw him as a contented man.

In the early Thirties the Great Depression was at its worst and consequently unemployment was very high. One knock-on effect of this was that the halls in Errol Street which were at the disposal of the guilds, fraternities, sodalities and associations of the great St Francis' church in Cumberland Street were busier than ever.

They had always been busy of an evening but throughout these dismal years they were busy not only in the afternoons but in the mornings as well. Young men and their elders played endless games of snooker and billiards. Card games abounded and although gambling was discouraged I think we can take it that it prevailed on occasion through all these activities although again we can take it that relative poverty ensured that the stakes were very small.

Out of this environment there grew an enquiry which grew to a demand that they should do something even without financial reward but something which would use their abundant free-time and stimulate their interest.

It was Jim and some other men of mature years who suggested they should form a football team. Such a team, it was argued, could play in the Juvenile Leagues. Were things to go well for them they might, just might, gain entry to one of the less fashionable leagues of Junior football.

For the more ambitious of these dreams to come to pass, they would need to be 'walled off' so that only those who paid for entry could see the matches.

My friend Jim Livingstone has a dictum that "everything takes longer than you think!" This was at its most valid in this instance. Firstly, a Committee had to be formed and — surprise, surprise — Jim Morrison was appointed as Secretary and a man who had been a trade union officer was made Chairman. Then a Constitution had to be written and approved. Then the quest for a site was started. What they wanted was land which was cheap yet not too far away from the centre of their activity. They realised that the solution possibly lay in the 'Maul's Mire', a huge and hugely unappealing tract of near wasteland which stretched from Polmadie in Glasgow to the western edges of Rutherglen. Most of it was dreadful but there were indicators that some serious activities were possible. There was a nine-hole golf course of indifferent standard which was controlled by a club with an annual subscription of half a guinea. Even more appropriately, there was a full-size football pitch with regulation goalposts and an ash playing surface.

Nevertheless, it was quickly recognised that there was no likelihood of their obtaining and using this facility. There were two obstacles. Firstly, the pitch was regularly used for matches of the Churches' League with teams formed from the membership of diverse churches and denominations within the Reformed tradition. The young men and their churches would not take kindly to their use of the pitch being whisked away from them. The second difficulty was that the pitch lay well below the height of the adjacent main road. Even enclosing the pitch would not stop non-paying spectators from standing by the road-side and watching the game 'for nothing'.

Yet all was not lost. Further enquiry concerning the Mire was deemed to be worthwhile if for no other reason than that they had no other road to travel.

So there they were. The Maul's Mire with all its horror of pools of stagnant water, with the slag deposits from Dixon's Ironworks brought in by a wee puggy train, with an old abandoned mine shaft with pathetic, worn, damaged signs warning of danger, with some elderly buddies living in total isolation and at its southern border the remnants of what was known as the 'Hundred Acre Dyke', beyond which lay Curtis Avenue and the rest of King's Park built by MacTaggart and Meikle, all that was their best bet. It was virtually their only bet.

But who owned the Mire and even more importantly, who was responsible for its administration?

Eventually they learned that the affairs of the Mire were handled by a firm of solicitors with premises up a close in St Enoch Square, a visit to which revealed that the Mire was administered in units of unequal size and importance. For example, there was a formal contract with Dixon's Blazes for the deposit of their waste in designated areas. There was, too, a not dissimilar formal agreement with the wee golf club and an arrangement with the Corporation of Glasgow for the marked improvement of the road through the Mire at Aikenhead Road to the city boundary but no similar agreement of the existing track from the boundary to the streets of Rutherglen. There was a pocket of land on the western side of the Mire and across Aikenhead Road from a row of miners' houses. The bit in the Mire consisted of a woe-begone house in a copse of pathetic trees which gave rise to a crop of crab apples. An elderly lady lived there. From time to time she would emerge to remonstrate with the boys who were climbing her trees or, in season, stealing her apples.

This wee site was yet another unit and a low annual charge imposed on the lady. Yet another unit was the football pitch used by the Church teams. It was handled by the senior partner, an active Christian and an Elder in an important church in Pollokshields. He had ordained that the church teams should pay a florin for each game played. This, of course, worked out at about a penny per player per game — not an arduous charge.

The new question at issue was whether there was another unit which would meet the requirements of the St Francis aspirants or — variant on a theme — was capable of being made suitable for them.

It is here or hereabouts that a word of warning should be inserted into this story. It should be remembered that when all this was happening I was still in primary school and even when much of it had come to fruition my age was measured in a single figure. Then again, years later, in my maturity, when I was discussing these matters with the survivors of these events, some of them were drifting into old age and experiencing the consequential loss of memory. But with these reservation duly noted, let us proceed.

Among other things, I recall being told that a well-meaning liar of possible good intent had put it to Jim that he should give himself a promotion which he never attained. More specifically, the advocate suggested that Jim should describe himself as Captain Jim Morrison. This, it was argued, would give him great martial bearing. Moreover, it worked well for Captain Hastings in the Agatha Christie novels about Poirot and his military associate.

To his credit, Jim would have none of it. Firstly, it was a lie and, secondly, were it to be exposed as an untruth it would rebound to the disadvantage of the whole venture.

Yet help was forthcoming from an unforeseen and unexpected source.

A partner in the law firm wrote to Jim and asked him to 'look in'. When he called he was advised that the religious senior partner had suggested that Mr Morrison and his group might just find that a particular unit, while not very inspiring, could be capable of 'improvement' and could therefore meet their needs. It was pointed out that this unit consisted of a very run-down house that had not been occupied for quite some time and, with the house, went a tract of land about three times more than they required, two-thirds of which consisted of a very severe slope down to a horrible 'manky' burn. For all that, there was a plateau in front of the house which could be transformed into a pitch suitable for the playing of football.

Jim was impressed and asked about the rent, which, it transpired would be a low nominal rent for three years. Jim was sufficiently alert to realise that after they had improved the site the rent would be increased for future years but he reckoned they would not be charged more than the wee golf course.

He said he would put it before their Committee who in turn 'bought it' and so it was that the embryonic, emerging football club took a massive step towards reality.

The tenancy having been offered and accepted by his Committee, Jim sent his three squads of workers into action.

The first squad was sent to work on the pathetic house. This team was made up of tradesmen and their unskilled and semi-skilled labourers. The roofers and slaters went in first using long ladders which had been made for the exercise. They were followed by bricklayers, stone-masons, and plasterers and shortly after them the plumbers, the joiners and decorators. The men worked extremely well and, remarkably quickly, the house could be decreed to be rain and wind-proof.

The next task was to redesign the edifice for use as a football pavilion. In this regard they had the pavilion at nearby Cathkin Park as their example. Baths had to be introduced and extra lavatorial facilities. Similarly, the kitchen arrangement had to undergo very considerable improvement.

At ground floor level three quite big rooms and one small one were laid out as were a bathroom of sorts and the extended kitchen. The largest room which was that nearest the door was set aside for the club officials and those of visiting teams. The two rooms of almost equal size were designated as the changing rooms for the two teams, while the small room was for the referee and the linesmen, if, that is, the latter two were provided. For some less important matches the linesmen were provided by the two clubs, an arrangement which almost invariably led to charge and counter-charges of partisanship and a lack of objectivity.

There had been no need to deploy electricians and gas-fitters. In Glasgow these utilities were, at that time, provided by the Corporation. The house had never had such facilities and the cost of providing them from the nearest junction points in Jessie Street, some 250 yards away, was regarded by the Committee as prohibitive. So far as lighting was concerned, it was argued that almost all their activities would be conducted in day-light and that oil lamps, strong torches and candles could be used as required. As for cooking, a large coal and wood-fired stove had been acquired and was by then safely installed in the refurbished kitchen.

Having ascertained that all was going well in and on the house – and having been gratified by reports from the tradesmen that they were thoroughly enjoying being back working with their tools – Jim and his Committee colleagues released and set to work the other two squads.

The second group was charged with laying out the plateau as an acceptable football pitch.

The first task was to make the ground level. Then they laid out and marked the pitch. The Committee had advised a playing surface of 130 yards by 88 yards. That made this park a shade broad (but well within the regulations). The Committee wanted breadth as they had tentative agreements with two nippy, speedy wingers. Once the playing surface was ready with regulatory goalposts and provision for nets, the workers turned their attention to a fence behind which the spectators would stand, the fence being destined to be treated as a crash-barrier on which spectators could lean.

The final task for that squad was to provide two tiers of stand provision around the park, but five tiers stretching for a little distance on both sides of the midway line. Such liberal provision for spectators was a shade ambitious, but there were to be cup-games where nearly all of it was called into action.

The final task was entrusted to the third squad which built a wooden frame to which they attached corrugated iron sheets which had to be painted. This fencing struck some folk as excessive but rightly or wrongly it was deemed prudent to encase the totality of the unit.

With all that achieved there were two other matters to clear. Firstly, they had to build a concrete block with three admission areas: as someone said at the time it was three 'turnstiles' without turnstiles. We all knew what he meant.

The final, final task was to provide a moderately impressive door into the park for 'Players and Officials', complete with a sign to that effect.

All this cost money. So the Committee set up a Sub-Committee. Its 'raison d'être' was to raise money but it would have been imprudent to say that, so it was called 'The Entertainment Committee'.

It did great work. It laid on concerts, dances, soirées, conversaziones, variety shows, a Christmas pantomime, a night of light opera selections, debates, gymnastic displays and an evening with the parochial choir. There were too the jumble sales, the 'bring and buy', a book and gramophone record sale and an afternoon tea dance. Money did not exactly pour in but it did flow in and amounted to a sum which paid for the materials used on the park, a thank you party for each squad and not one, not two, but three sets of 'strips' for the team and three balls.

There then arose the questions of who would 'open' the Park. A lot of folk favoured a member of the hierarchy but Jim argued in favour of a sports personality.

Sir Ian Colquhoun, a Baronet based on Loch Lomondside (the estate now being an international golf course) had made a name for himself in the Olympics. So Jim won that debate and then wrote to Colquhoun and on the day he arrived, he did a neat smart job, signed autographs, waved — and went back to Luss. This attracted more, much more Press coverage — almost certainly more than had it been a Bishop or even an Archbishop.

There remained but one issue.

Against whom would they play?

Here there was an event of great importance – for them!! A Junior Club in a mining village or small town in Ayrshire, which played in the Western Junior League announced that they were 'bust' and would not be playing in the forthcoming season.

Jim wrote immediately. His Club, he wrote, was ready to go, had a ground and a strip and was financially solvent. They – officials and players – were ready to deputise.

They were accepted.

As I recall it, that was for season 1934-35 or 1935-36.

And how did they fare? Well now, the answer to that is 'not too badly'.

Jim was a firm believer in the spine system, as were Glasgow Rangers.

The system was that a team should have a firm spine up the middle of the park – a good goal-keeper, a strong, effective centre-half and a quick effective centre-forward. In the case of Rangers this was exemplified in the Thirties by Gerry Dawson in goal, Meiklejohn at centre-half and Thornton or Jimmy Smith at centre-forward.

Jim was fortunate in that he had a particularly good goal-keeper. This was a big broad yet very agile man called Heggarty who lived in a rather fine red sand-stone building in Albert Road which was directly across the road from Crosshill Railway Station. This house was a five-apartment flat and was regarded by the rest of the team as an indicator of affluence.

Up front he had 'Fatsy' Bagan. True, he was rather rotund but he was a very effective poacher-type centre-forward. Moreover, with his body shape he had a low centre of gravity with the result he was not easily knocked off the ball. On top of that he could fall with conviction and lured many a referee into giving him, and the team, a penalty kick, while on his own he was a prolific scorer — provided he received good service. The inside forwards were undistinguished but they had two excellent wingers, one called McAloon and the other McArdle. Both had been 'senior' players, one with Celtic and the other with Celtic and then with Hamilton Academicals. Both had been 'reinstated' to play in the Junior ranks. A recurring debate within the core support was which was the better player of the two.

Where Jim's 'spine' theory was vulnerable was that they did not have a good centre-half. They did have Jimmy Dempsey, who was regarded as a versatile right wing-half who could play moderately effectively at right-back or centre-half. He had had trials for Third Lanark who pronounced that he was good — but not good enough. Furthermore, the difficulty in playing him at centre-half was that other teams 'sussed' that he was not a natural central defender and exposed this short-coming. When Jim and his colleagues played Dempsey at centre-half they had to reconcile themselves to the opposition scoring at least twice. What they had to do was pray that 'Fatsy' Bagan could score a hat-trick.

When the going got tough on the financial side there was a belief that 'Fatsy' was paid in Woodbine cigarettes.

In their first full season they settled a little below mid-point in the league, about a third from the bottom and two-thirds from the top. In one season, however, they surprised themselves and finished fourth or fifth in the league.

Then in the wake of that achievement there came two great events.

The first of these almost certainly involved chicanery.

The Central League was a very prestigious collection of Junior football teams. As I recall it the other local Junior team, Shawfield, played in that League, as did Petershill, Benburb, Rutherglen Glencairn, Pollok, Athurlie, St Anthony's and the great St. Roch's. These clubs had impressive grounds and, even more importantly, impressive support, frequently attracting bigger attendance than that of the Senior clubs in the Lower Division of the Senior game.

The Central League had a provision that to gain admission to their ranks, clubs in other leagues e.g. the Western, had to 'stand down' i.e. not play for a whole season and then and only then apply for admission to the Central League — all without any guarantee of the application being successful. This was a deterrent to 'see off' the pretentious.

Yet notwithstanding all of this, quite suddenly it was announced that Jim's wee team had been dissolved whereupon like a phoenix from the ashes there emerged a 'new' club, with a 'new' name: Greyfriars F.C. was born.

It just so happened that they played at Friary Park, that they had the same colours and the same strip as that which had been dissolved. Moreover, the Committee was much the same as that under 'the ancien régime'. They had merely moved around as folk do at a whist drive. Jim was no longer Secretary: he was Chairman.

I had a friend of sorts, John Currie, who lived in the house above ours. His father was a member of the Committee of Shawfield Juniors. John understandably charged the old St. Francis' club, my uncle Jim and me with cheating.

My riposte was weak: it was for the Central League to decide and they had decided in our favour.

The other matter was even more dramatic. 'Uncle Jim's wee team' won three cups in the one week.

The first of the three, the Smyllum Cup, was won on a Tuesday evening. It was not much of a Cup. It was run to help finance a pathetic Catholic Charity in the Borders where they provided work and a sparse living for unemployed men irrespective of religious affiliation, if any.

Only eight clubs competed. One victory and you were semi-finalists. It was generally won by either St. Anthony's in Govan or St. Roch's in Garngad.

That year Jim's lot won it.

The second cup, one of the less prestigious cups offered by local newspapers, was won on the Thursday evening.

It was the third that was impressive. As I recall it, the cup was linked to either the *Evening Times* or the *Evening News*. It was generally won by one of the stronger teams in the Central League.

As luck had it, the finalists were the local rivals, Shawfield and Greyfriars. Moreover, the final was to be played on the Saturday afternoon at Shawfield Stadium, the home of Clyde F.C.

The game attracted a crowd of about 15,000. Greyfriars had never before played to so many people.

Both teams scored in the first half so it was 'one each' at half-time.

Out of the blue 'Fatsy' Bagan scored a poacher's goal, giving Greyfriars a 2–1 lead.

Most of the spectators were supporting or favouring Shawfield and their roars were impressive. So too was the response of the Shawfield players who strove earnestly to score an equalising goal and so take the game to extra time.

Wave after wave of their red jerseys came pouring into the Greyfriars penalty box.

Heggarty, in goal, was magnificent.

The Greyfriars defenders were almost out on their feet.

Then with three minutes to go, centre-half Dempsey thumped the ball up the park towards the side-line. He was clearly hoping for a throw-in and a moment's respite.

But his intention was thwarted, for McAloon, who was hovering just near the mid-line, collected the ball and like the hare in the dog track made for the corner flag at the Shawfield end. We surmised he was hoping to waste some time up there or try to win a corner off a defender. He then spotted 'Fatsy' running up the middle. But McAloon still had to control the ball, and 'Fatsy', who had only to run, realised he was too far ahead so he turned to come back a bit.

At that point McAloon chose to cross the ball which hit 'Fatsy' on his left buttock and with a ricochet flew from 'Fatsy' Bagan's lower torso into the back of the net. Greyfriars were winning 3–1. In effect they had won.

Some of the Shawfield defenders protested but the referee just stood and shrugged. It was a valid goal.

And that is how Greyfriars won that cup and won their three cups in a week.

The local press made a lot of it. One journalist writing in an evening paper said: "With a few minutes to go, Bagan, a terrific terrier of a player, scored the concluding goal by a brilliant header. It caused perplexity in the press box as we could not comprehend how he managed to position his head so low that it could connect with the incoming cross from McAloon."

There were, too, the down days. These were the days when they lost 5–0 and, on another occasion, were defeated 7–1, a mini-disaster experienced not only by Jim's wee team but later by the mighty and proud Glasgow Rangers. Moreover, down days extended to such occasions as having two men ordered off by the referee and the day playing Cadder Juniors in Cadder when the home team went ahead with the solitary goal of the game and thereafter kicked the ball into the nearby canal. Each time it was retrieved it emerged heavier than before and at shies players could barely lift it over their heads far less throw it any distance. At goal-kicks the two goal-keepers could barely kick it out of the penalty box.

Such 'down' days extended to days of very low attendance. I remember vividly a day they were at home to Glasgow Perthshire. It was a day of cloud at zero feet. The world seemed to be covered by misty wet conditions. Visibility levels were in doubt and it would have been merciful had the referee 'abandoned' the game.

But he didn't. With ten minutes to go before the start of the game Uncle Jim was very angry. At that time the total paying attendance was three – and two of them were regulars who were close friends of Jim.

Jim maintained he had been assured by hundreds (possibly 15–20 folk) that they would come. He directed me to go and look for them and on seeing them, to run back and report.

I went out and positioned myself on top of the coal-bins, peering into the mist. At first nothing moved. Then out of the mist there emerged a man with no coat but with the collar of his jacket turned up for a protection of sorts from the elements.

Foolishly, stupidly, I regarded him as the vanguard of a host to follow. I reported this to my uncle Jim who thereupon took command of the situation. "You three lads to your posts," he cried. Whereupon the three gate-men went to their booths, one to the sixpenny gate, one to the fourpenny unemployed gate and one to the twopenny pensioners' and boys' gate. Each man fingered his roll of admission tickets, prepared to pull along the perforated line.

The man of the turned-up collar arrived. He ignored the three manned entrances and confidently strode to and rapped on the gate marked 'players and officials' and when the door was cautiously opened he pushed it wide open. "Scout for Accrington Stanley," he announced to the world — and came in for nothing!

At the time of the kick-off the paying attendance had crept up to 8.

Such then were the days of what the ladies in the family – all five of them – referred to as 'Jim's wee team'.

It was a casualty of the Second World War.

It did not last beyond 1941. Almost the entire playing squad went into the Forces – some as volunteers, some as conscripts. The Committee members were all by then back at work. Jim in the Ministry of Labour was working twelve hours of overtime every week.

In the post-war years the Maul's Mire was transformed.

Firstly, the landscape was levelled. Glasgow Corporation arranged for public sector housing to be erected. Shops, churches and Scout halls and the like opened. Lanarkshire County Council did much the same on their side of the boundary.

More recently, yet further changes have come about. The site of the house of the lady with the crab-apples is now an Asda Supermarket. Across the road is a brand-new Indoors Sports Centre with a full-size football pitch where two of my grandchildren referee games.

The site of Friary Park and the house where the volunteer tradesmen worked is now a facility of the Local Authority Cleansing department. It has a dump in which householders and others discard a remarkable variety of possessions.

The pitch where the churches' teams played is now a slip-road from the M74.

The area is now known as Toryglen. That nomenclature did not come from nowhere: it was the name of the original wee golf club and, of course, the wee golf club, too, has gone.

Visitors would never know from what is there now, that this was once the mire of stinking streams, slag deposits and small coal bings.

But when I am there I hear the roars of the excited support on their better days and I think of Uncle Jim's wee team and in particular the glorious week in which they won three cups.

Activities of the Elderly

This short tale is derived from an interview on BBC Radio 4.

The lady being interviewed was an author and at the time of the interview was in her middle nineties. My unreliable memory tells me she was Doris Lessing. The other lady, the interviewer, came over as being in her early to middle fifties.

Most of the time was taken up discussing novels written by the older lady and others.

As the interviewer worked her way towards a conclusion she seemed to adopt a somewhat lofty, superior tone.

"You are retired now," she pronounced and hurried on. "What do you do all day? Do you garden? Do you listen to music? Do you watch television? Do you have friends who call? Do you paint? What do you do all day? How do you spend your days?"

It was clear that the author was offended.

"Look you here, young lady," she responded. "Let me tell you that being elderly is very hard work. One has to run to hospitals and clinics and doctors and nurses in order that one can run yet again to hospitals and clinics and doctors and nurses. It is very hard work, very hard work indeed."

Bob McCrae's Tale of the St Andrews Caddy

I was inclined to say that this story was Bob McCrae's story, but as Bob would readily have admitted, he was told the story by another man – a former club champion of Cathcart Castle Golf Club.

Yet it would be wrong to brush Bob aside too readily.

Bob had been a telegram boy, one of an army of teen-age lads who — in their uniforms, including the pill-box hat — delivered telegrams throughout the cities of the U.K. Most such lads were promoted to Postal and Telegraph officers, lots of them in time deployed as counter staff in large Post Offices.

Robert was one of seven or eight such young men, who, on release from the Forces, sat an examination and in the event of success moved from the Post Office to the more traditional Civil Service.

Bob came to the Ministry of Labour which is where I met him and, through him, I came to know his two close friends from their telegram days. Hugh Brown went to the Ministry of Pensions and National Insurance, but went on to be the Labour M.P. for the Provan Division of Glasgow. The other was Bill Lauder, who became the owner of an estate by the Sound of Mull — though that is a story for another time.

Bob had a good career in the Ministry of Labour. He was almost promoted in 1954 and was promoted in 1955. Further promotion came in 1961 and he finished his years in the Department as a Senior Executive Officer and Manager of Motherwell Employment Exchange, by which time he was an M.B.E.

In his retirement he lived in East Kilbride and joined Bonnington Moor Golf Club as an associate member. This entitled him to play during the week when the course was quiet but not at weekends when the course was busy.

One day he played a round with a fellow associate member who in his day had been champion at Cathcart Castle. It was over a drink at the nineteenth hole that the Cathcart Castle man told this story to Bob, who, at the first opportunity, relayed it to me.

One time in the twenties of the last century he and a colleague from Cathcart Castle had been playing in a four-ball foursome competition at St. Andrews. The event had been sponsored by a Glasgow newspaper.

The Cathcart duo had won their morning match, but it had not been resolved until they were on the 21st green. Happily victorious as they were, they had to trek back to the markers who told them that they had twenty minutes to grab a sandwich or two, a glass of milk, visit the gents' and be on the first tee to start their afternoon match.

When they arrived at the starting point they found there was only one caddy left. He looked extremely elderly. He was stooped and his long grey hair tumbled beyond his shoulders.

The Cathcart men quickly agreed they could not ask him to carry two bags. They would have him caddy for one man for the first nine holes, and switch to the other man for the second nine.

When they were about the seventh or eighth hole and approaching the 'turn', one ball went into quite thick rough. As the three of them were walking, kicking the grass in search of the ball, the narrator started talking to the caddy.

"Did you play yourself?"

"Aye, ah did, ah did."

"Were you any good?"

"Aye, well, no' bad."

"Did you enter competitions and the like?"

"Aye, ah did, ah did."

"Did you win anything?"

"Aye, noo and again, like."

"What was the best thing you ever won?"

"The British Open."

And he did too. I remember that at the time that Bob McCrae told me this tale we knew the caddy's name. I looked it up in the Guinness Book of Records. He had won it in the late years of the nineteenth century. His score was higher than those ahead of him and of those who came after. I guessed that his victory had been during a spell of high winds to which he had adapted better than his opponents.

I once told this tale at a dinner party in the home of Helen Liddell, otherwise the Right Honourable Baroness Liddell of Cartdyke. I was rewarded with gales of laughter.

So Helen told her tale. She told of a day in the Lords. She had promised the Labour Whips she would vote and support the Party view. But she was running late and as she scurried along the corridor found herself at the back of a very elderly Peer hobbling along on two sticks.

Fortunately they both made it.

With the vote over they talked as they walked slowly back to the Chamber.

She asked: "Have you been in the House for a long time?"

"A very long time."

"Did you come in from politics or were you in business or industry or the Arts perhaps?"

"I was a politician," he observed.

"And did you hold office?"

"Yes — now and again."

Helen smiled. "What was the highest office you ever held?" she asked.

"Viceroy of India," he quietly answered.

Had there been an umpire in attendance he would, I think, have declared: "Game, set and match to Baroness Liddell."

Huvvin' Fun

This story concerns a bunch of lads who were all of an age and who were apprentice engineers in a factory in Jessie Street off Polmadie Road.

Although all seven or eight of the boys were involved, this tale is dominated by two particular lads. *In extremis,* it comes over as a sort of western movie. One lad tends to be seen as the hero, wearing a white jacket and a white hat and riding a white horse, whilst the pest of the piece can be construed as the villain with an unshaven face, a dark shirt, a black hat and riding a black horse which he treats badly.

The 'good' lad was certainly different from the others. His name was Maxwell Erskine and he did not live locally as did all the others. He lived in Mosspark, a very fine 'up-market' housing estate. In his private life he was active in both the Youth Fellowship and the Boys' Brigade at his local Presbyterian Church. His other midweek activity was attending evening classes in what at the time was the Royal College of Science and Technology.

The other major role was taken by Abraham Abernethy Dewar, known to his family, his limited coterie of friends and his apprentice colleagues as Abe – shades of President Lincoln, though he was markedly less principled than the President.

Abe knew that Maxie Erskine was cleverer than he was, that he was more industrious and eager to give their employers good service. It was not that Abe avoided work. He did what he had to do and did it with acceptable competence but he never went the extra mile. From time to time, Abe told the other lads that Maxie was a 'sook', that he would do anything to ingratiate himself with higher paid help.

It was evident to the rest of the lads that there was no love lost between Maxie and Abe. Maxie chose to avoid Abe as much as he could while Abe never lost an opportunity to do Maxie down and this final act was the all-time confirmation of that.

One day it transpired that it was Maxie's birthday.

"Great," cried Abe, "we'll gie him his birthday bumps at dinner time. Right?" No-one demurred.

By long-standing convention no work was done in the factory from 12.30 to 1.30. There was a canteen and most of the adult employees availed themselves of its facilities. Of the apprentices only Maxie and another lad went to the canteen. All the other lads including Abe brought 'pieces' – sandwiches of varying thickness where the recurring 'fillings' were cold sausages, cold meat – particularly corned beef – and cheese.

On the day of Maxie's birthday Abe saw to it that when Maxie and his companion came out of the canteen, he was grabbed and hustled outside. A large piece of canvas had been obtained. Most of the lads grabbed the edges of the canvas and held it at knee-height.

"Birthday Bumps!" shouted Abe and he and two others threw Maxie on to the canvas. This they then lifted up and down till they could throw Maxie up a few feet and catch him as he started to fall. As this continued they gradually reduced the level at which they caught him. Originally it had been level with their wrists, then their thighs, then their knees till it was at calf-muscle height. "Wan mair!" cried Abe and they threw Max in the air. "Lower still!" cried Abe as they threw Max in the air. "Lower still!" cried Abe and the boys prepared to catch at ankle height but to be effective the canvas had to be held taut. It wasn't. One boy sneezed and let go his hold. The canvas slanted towards the ground. The weight of Max's body took most of the canvas to ground level so there was no slack. In effect he landed on the ground and did so with a sickening thud.

"Come oan, then," cried Abe, "get up!"

"I can't," said Max.

"Stoap the kiddin'," demanded Abe, "get up!"

"I can't," repeated Max.

Somebody fetched the First Aid man from the canteen. On

examining Max he phoned for an ambulance. As the ambulance sped away, the 1.30 bell called the rest back to work.

One of the foremen was a man called John Scott. He was an excellent engineer and knew Maxie's father.

Not slow to act, he made a point of accosting Abe.

"What the hell did you lot think you were doing? Did you not know it was dangerous?"

"Whit ur ye oan aboot?" replied Abe. "We were just huvvin' fun. Sno' oor fault he goat a wee bit hurted, like. He'll be back ramorra moarnin – jist wait and see."

But he was not back the next morning. The tragedy was that Maxie was never back. It took time to ascertain the severity of the damage and the likelihood, if any, of recovery.

Max, it was eventually learned, was paralysed from his neck to his toes.

His father was of high standing in the Masonic Order.

His attention was drawn to an excellent well-run Masonic nursing home in Yorkshire. The authorities agreed to take his son.

Years and years passed. John Scott had retired and the man who replaced him had retired. His successor was in poor health and there was talk of his going early.

One day at Scott's instigation he and Maxie's father met in town. "I wanted to see you and to let you know that yon clown Dewar is to be the next foreman in my old section. I wanted you to hear it from me."

There was a pause and he went on.

"You must be very resentful."

Mr Erskine looked both sad and thoughtful.

"No, John," he pronounced, "I am not resentful. You know, John, that I am no papist but yon St Augustine of theirs got it right. He argued that resentment is pointless. In fact, John, he compared it to taking poison and hoping another man will die. No, John, I am not resentful. I'm just sad, very sad. Will you have another, John?"

The Boy from the Next Close

This is a true story. So too are many of the others but in this case it is prudent to use only one name. The second character – and there are only two of them – remains, as the title indicates, as the boy from the adjoining close.

Murdo McKinlay was the seventh son of a seventh son. Legend would have it that he would be an eminent piper. Maybe he should have been – but he wasn't. His family however argued that he had another Celtic attribute: second-sight.

Yet Murdo, himself, knew that was not quite right. He could not foretell events but he knew he had an exceptional ability. Some people could read 'body-language' better than others. For his part Murdo knew that he had exceptional ability in this regard. The merest glance, the most fleeting of expressions, could reveal a good deal to Murdo.

This was not all a blessing to Murdo. For example there were occasions when he would have preferred not to know what his wife was really thinking.

One day while standing at the window he noticed the boy from the next close come out and cross to the nearby bus-stop. Murdo scowled and turning to his wife said: "That boy is trouble, serious trouble. Don't ask me what kind of trouble – I do not know but it will be serious, very serious. Don't ask me how I know because I do not know. It is just something I sense."

Three years later Murdo and his wife and family moved and lived in a suburb, still part of the conurbation but outside the city limits.

Some six or seven years later Murdo's wife mentioned that the *Herald*, the local broad-sheet, had a piece about a murder in a park which they had used while living in their old house. The newspaper article was supplemented by a wee map indicating where the body had been found. The McKinlays knew it well.

Before a week was out the *Herald* carried a further piece. Two locals – young men in their early twenties – had been arrested and charged with the murder. One of them was 'the boy from the next close'.

Five months elapsed before the case came for trial. The prosecution case was that the victim had been lured to a hidden area for immoral purposes whereupon he had been thumped by the other. A defence of sorts was advanced but the jury acted with remarkable expedition.

The verdict was an item on the Scottish News as the McKinlays were having their tea. The wife poured her husband's second cup of tea and asked: "But, Murdo dear, how did you know?"

"That I don't know, but I am the seventh son of a seventh son."

Mrs McKinlay looked thoughtful.

"Thank God we have just the two boys," she said, and poured her own second cup of tea.

Discontented Comrades

There is a phenomenon which is known by and experienced by many folk in administration, in business, in the Forces, in higher education, in schools, in certain churches and in all sorts of other organisations. The phenomenon is that of the deviant group.

All these organisations accept people in blocks – new recruits for the Forces, new intakes to specific courses in Higher Education, new groups of apprentices or trainees in Industry, new seminarians in some Churches.

Year after year they do it and year after year all goes well, and then, for no apparent reason, a new intake does not conform. Instead it is non-conformist, it is querulous, just difficult.

There is no one term for this experience. Those in the Forces tend to speak of 'the awkward squad'. Others speak of 'a difficult bunch', some refer to 'a wobbly lot'.

There are two difficulties here — the nomenclature and the inability to account for the errant.

The normal reaction when experienced is to swear, kick the cat, and grapple and live with the situation as best one can.

Those of us entrusted with the S.T.U.C. Summer School, one summer in the middle of the seventies, had our experience of this phenomenon.

Labour had been in power from 1964 to 1970. Ted Heath and his Conservative colleagues were in command from 1970 until 1974 when Wilson and his team came back in office.

As I recall it, all went well with the Summer School throughout most if not all of these years. When there were hiccups they were of our own making. Then we got a very different intake. It was not too bad over the first weekend but by the Tuesday morning lecturers and tutors were beginning to exchange experiences and by Tuesday afternoon we were being inundated with complaints and critical comments from those entrusted with the teaching.

Then came the Wednesday. My recollection was that we were due to be joined by a distinguished lecturer, none other than Hughie Scanlan, the fiery leader of the Engineers' Union. On the Tuesday evening some of us dared to predict that Scanlan would not arrive: he would, we argued, send a deputy. Come the day we were vindicated. Scanlan was not coming, we were told. He had arranged to send a substitute who, as I recall it, was a Mr Foster.

On the day itself a member of the S.T.U.C. staff, acting as Chairman, explained the situation and introduced the speaker. Scanlan would have been fiery. His replacement was a furnace. He was very critical of the Labour Government and concluded by urging his audience to have nothing to do with the Incomes Policy which was a key policy of the Government.

In the ensuing Question and Discussion period I suggested that he had a cheek arguing as he did. He was with us, I asserted, because Scanlan was deployed elsewhere. Indeed, as Foster was denouncing Incomes Policy, Scanlan, together with other Trade Union Leaders, was in Downing Street for beer and sandwiches to discuss the Incomes Policy.

The intervention on my part was immediately denounced. Various speakers told me I had been discourteous to 'a very distinguished guest'.

By the afternoon session we had ample evidence of discontent which was being channelized quite effectively. Attendance at the lectures, seminars and the like fell to 50% at best.

By the Thursday we were being told that some delegates were going home and that our programme had been rubbish from the beginning.

Some three weeks or so after the end of the School I received a letter, not inviting me, but summoning me to attend a post-mortem on what had gone wrong.

Telephone calls confirmed that all lecturers and tutors (but not Mr Foster) had received identical peremptory letters. It also transpired that the S.T.U.C. had received some 15–20 letters of complaint from dissatisfied comrades, some suggesting that the whole operation had been a defence of the Capitalist system.

Come the day, three members of the General Council who had been entrusted with conducting 'the hearing' arrived ten minutes late: they had been out for lunch on the strength of our being due to be grilled. They were led by Andy Forman of U.S.D.A.W., the shop-workers' union. One of the other two was a teacher from the Educational Institute of Scotland.

Once they had settled themselves we, the recipients of the summonses, were brought in. We entered in descending order of deemed importance. First was Jimmy Milne, the Deputy General Secretary of the S.T.U.C. Next was a man called Monaghan who was an old hand and who was a Senior Lecturer at Strathclyde University. Then I took third position and after me came Helen Liddell (now the Rt. Hon. Baroness Liddell of Cartdyke), at that time an economist with the S.T.U.C. and so it went on till we were all in and seated.

"This is a very serious matter," pronounced Andy Forman, not preceding it with any thanks for coming.

"We have received a lot of correspondence. There has been a great deal of discontent. We must know what went wrong."

"What do you have to say, Mr Deputy Secretary?" He glanced at Jimmy Milne.

"The students did not like what they were being taught." At that he stopped.

"And what were they taught?" demanded Forman.

"The programme approved by you and the other members of the General Council," answered Milne.

"And they didn't like it?" exploded Forman.

"That's what I understood you to say, comrade Chairman," replied Milne.

"Do you know what they did want to learn?" asked the temporary Chairman.

"Yes, I think so," said Milne.

"Well, man, do not hesitate. Spit it out."

"Well," said Milne, "one cannot be certain but I reckon what they really wanted to know was how to strip down and then re-assemble a Kalashnikov!"

A very long silence ensued. Forman looked at his two colleagues but did not speak. Eventually, he said: "Well…, I suppose that finishes that."

"I would have thought so," said Milne and as the 'top table' rose and gathered their papers, so did we.

Normal relations were restored the ensuing year and continued in my experience until the last of my involvement.

Desmond O'Connor

Desmond O'Connor was an Irishman with a somewhat justified air of distinction. It is said that Irishmen are much suited to four occupations – Priests, Publicans, Politicians and Poets. Desmond was none of these. He was an engineer and that was common enough in the Black North with men of Scottish stock but Desmond was of the Celtic tradition, as his name suggested. But how he became an engineer was far from clear.

As a boy he lived in a Dublin suburb and being bright found himself in a Christian Brothers' School. The Christian Brothers, as an Order, had a reputation for strict discipline and any deviation from good behaviour and an anxiety to learn resulted in corporal punishment on a severe scale. Despite his mannerly disposition Desmond found himself, again and again, at the receiving end of that zeal.

This experience led to disenchantment – not with learning but with active membership of the Church. Yet although he was a personal critic of Mother Church he could, like Henry VIII as a young man, be its defender. I remember being with him at a University event when a man passed a most derogatory remark about Catholicism. Desmond flicked the ash off his cigar, looked the man in the eye and said: "It served my parents very well." He then ignored any riposte and turned to me to engage in general conversation.

But I am in danger of rushing ahead of myself.

When Desmond was a young man in the middle twenties his friends started acquiring bicycles. As they did so and became more proficient in their deployment, they increasingly cycled and asked Desmond to buy a bike and join them. Eventually he succumbed whereupon something strange and totally unforeseen occurred: within six or eight weeks of acquiring his first bicycle, Desmond was more competent in the handling and deployment of the bike than were his friends.

In the fullness of time he and some of the others joined a proper cycling club and they found that when races were held Desmond was frequently the winner. When he was not victorious he was generally second or third. No one else had that consistency.

The outcome was that he was chosen for the Irish Free State Cycling Team for the Empire Games in 1930. Come the games he won a Bronze medal for being third in a final.

That success was to change his life.

Some two or three months after his success in the Games, Desmond was approached by an agent for an International Cycling Circus. As the name suggested this organisation and its cyclists toured the world. Their shows always started with trick cyclists performing all sorts of remarkable acts, but each show culminated with an International Race with men representing 12-15/16 countries. They spent six weeks to two months touring Britain and Ireland, then another two months in the USA, Canada and in some years Mexico.

Thereafter it was New Zealand, Australia, and South Africa and Rhodesia, then Cairo, Naples, Rome, Barcelona, Marseilles and up through France and Germany to the Benelux countries and Scandinavia with the tour always finishing in Norway. After Norway they came back to London and were 'stood down' for some six to eight weeks, whereupon they reassembled and started all over again.

Desmond was impressed by the overall efficiency of the organisation and never ceased to admire how either the entrepreneur or Almighty God arranged it that as often as not he and his Free State Tricolour would win in Liverpool, Dublin, Galway and Cork – and in due course Boston, whereas he always lost and lost badly in Belfast. His French colleague won a lot in France, French-speaking Belgium, in Quebec and New Orleans. The German always seemed to do well in Germany and the Mid-West of the USA. The Scot did well in Toronto and parts of Australia. The other thing Desmond told me was that he banked £10,000 a year from 1931 to 1939 when it came to an end.

Desmond O'Connor came into the life of the University when he married Mary Reid who was on the teaching staff of one of our smaller departments. Mary had been married before but it had not worked out. It was said that her first husband who had owned a successful business had exercised his own variation on, or version of 'le droit du seigneur.' Mary was disenchanted and so that marriage ended.

After some years as the young divorcee she found herself on the Saturday of a Glasgow holiday weekend in the backroom of a pub in Girvan where a sing-song was well under way. Desmond and some friends came in and that was that. There were and are those who maintained it was 'one enchanted evening' stuff i.e. that their eyes had met 'across a crowded room' and the rest was inevitable.

There was some 15 years or so between them and others argued that Desmond saw himself as a protector rather than as amorous husband. Be that as it may, whatever the nature of the relationship, it seemed to satisfy both of them.

There was an incident during the war which revealed another man's evaluation of Desmond.

He and a team of 15 men from Ireland were working as civil engineers aboard a British battleship in Scapa Flow. News came through that a German pocket battleship had made a dash for the open seas. The battleship on which Desmond was working and another craft in Scapa Flow were ordered to lift anchor and go to sea in open pursuit. The captain sent for Desmond. He explained that they were sailing towards possible combat. Were he and his team to be taken prisoner life could be very rough and difficult. He, the captain, said he was willing to swear them all into the Royal Navy so that they would have the protection of the Geneva Convention. It was, however, an all or nothing situation: he was not prepared to do some and not others and he was not prepared to let each man vote. It was for Desmond to decide – in or out.

Desmond said they would go for the Royal Navy

On their being enrolled in the ranks, Desmond became a full lieutenant and the two foremen became CPOs, the rest were ratings.

When Desmond died Mary who was a fairly regular churchgoer drew on the services of her Minister for the funeral service. He said Des had been an engineer, was very 'handy' around the house and did a lot of 'do it yourself'.

It was a pathetic address for a man who deserved so much better.

Comrade Ivanov

This story, like some of the others, concerns events at and others arising from the S.T.U.C. Summer School. For once I remember what happened and do so with reasonable clarity. What I cannot recall with the same precision is when it occurred, yet I do remember that it happened during the three, four, five year run when we were not at the University of Stirling or at that of St Andrews. During this phase we were at a former private residence – it was called Treebank – at the end of a heavily wooded driveway and located about the southern edge of Kilmarnock. This property had been acquired by the S.T.U.C. itself or by some other left-wing organisation. As I saw it, the reasoning which had led to the purchase had been muddled and that is to be both polite and kind. It appeared it had been bought for use by week-end schools, mini-conferences, working parties and in-house Trade Union staff training and other tuition. It all had a superficial logic but took no cognizance of the economies of scale: put bluntly, there was not enough of that type of business at competitive prices to see it heavily used throughout the year. That was the point on which the Universities scored. Moreover, the Universities could maintain their support staff throughout the year whereas the Kilmarnock venture, as I understood it, was either laying folk off and then re-engaging them or keeping them on out of sentiment even though some were then fairly seriously under-occupied.

It was against this background that someone on the General Council of the S.T.U.C. argued that by sending the Summer School to a University the Labour Movement was 'leaking money' which could be spent within the Movement by sending the Summer School to the Kilmarnock facility.

The down-side to all this soon became apparent. In the Kilmarnock house students and tutors had to share rooms. Worse: the place was too small for the Annual Summer School. Then again, it had no University ambience to rub off on the students. There were yet other gripes but the General Council had decreed and we had to survive and provide as best we could. Yet, as suggested, the deficiencies were manifest and it was remarkable that Kilmarnock prevailed as long as it did.

In the year of the story Ben Smith of NALGO, a vehement anti-Communist, and I shared a room — as did two dedicated and devoted Communists, an economist also called Smith and a man of middle-class extraction called Harrison who was an employee of the S.T.U.C. The two teams were destined to joust — and joust we did!

The drama which we were fated to experience started with the arrival – unforeseen and unannounced – of Comrade Ivan Ivanov and his entourage of six 'minders'. Ivanov, we were told, was an important trade unionist in Bulgaria. More, he was a devoted admirer of and enthusiastic student of the works of Robert Burns, to whom he referred as 'our worker-poet'. He was in Britain, something he found to be extremely distasteful, on a cultural exchange visit.

While he was here, a left-wing Executive member of one of our 'unskilled' unions was cavorting round Bulgaria watching traditional folk-dancing and drinking tolerable Bulgarian wine to fortify himself for his supposedly delightful experience.

Finding himself in Scotland, Ivan had insisted on breaking away from his planned itinerary in order to visit Burns's Cottage outside Ayr. On hearing of this about-to-be-implemented wish the S.T.U.C. had insisted that he and his companions should be their guests and spend two nights at Treebank and by way of a reciprocal gesture he would tell the Summer School of the achievements and aspirations of the Socialist Trade Unionists of Bulgaria. He was, we were told, of such generosity of the spirit that he would even take questions and provide answers.

When Harrison told the tutors about this disruption to our programme I pointed out that this would involve the scrapping of an entire morning's programme. Harrison pronounced this was nonsense, not least as Comrade Ivanov planned to speak for only 50 minutes and take a few questions. It would, he assured us, be all over by the time of the morning coffee break. I argued that this was poppy-cock and nonsense: folk like Ivanov were incapable of speaking for less than two hours.

Finding accommodation for Ivan and his support team wasn't easy. It involved decanting eight students out of their rooms and squeezing them in with other students. Meanwhile, Ben Smith was arguing with me that two of Ivan's minders would be KGB agents. Even Ivan would not know which of the other five was his colleague.

Come the morning, Ivan was straining at the bit like the favourite in the trap at a greyhound meeting. He started exactly on time, doing so with the air of a man who had much to convey.

"Good morning, comrades," he started and went on: "My name is Ivanov, Ivan Ivanov, and I have the privilege and pleasure of being the Director of the Trade Union Centre in Sofia in Bulgaria. Unlike you in your decadent west we have no unemployment in Bulgaria. The constitution of our Socialist and Workers' Republic guarantees not only the right to work but a job to go with that right. In the event of a worker becoming redundant, a Committee, consisting of representatives of the management, the State and the workers' trade union, co-operate and work enthusiastically to find another job for the worker – frequently in the same factory or plant, occasionally in a near-by location and sometimes somewhere else."

So it went on for an hour and three-quarters.

When we got to questions, Harrison, who was in the Chair, chose sycophantic questioners who of course gave rise to safe, ingratiating supposed questions. "Do the people of Bulgaria want peace?" "Are trade union subscriptions high or low in Bulgaria?" "Would I be right in thinking that the Bulgarian workers are very worried about the high American expenditure on armaments?"

In choosing the questioners Harrison kept avoiding a Glasgow lad called Jim McTeague. Eventually Jim broke in: "Ur ye gonnae take ma question or ur ye no gonnae let me in? Dae ye hufty be a Communist tae get asking a question?"

This last query provoked considerable laughter. In his ensuing embarrassment Harrison eventually indicated that McTeague could put his.

"Right then," opened Jim. "It's aboot this Committee like what rummages aboot tae find ra guy another joab. You didnae say it but it seems this other joab can be quite faur away like – maybe even hunners o' miles away. Whit aboot the lad no' wantin' the other job? Efter aw, he might be merrit and ra wife wantin' tae stay near her mammy or he might want to stay and support a local fitba club or he might huv a wee bird who sees him right noo un again or he might just like a local pub because aw his pals go there and he likes the crack. Whit then? Can he tell them whit tae dae with the job they offered him? Eh, whit happens then, like?" And to roars of laughter and approval he sat down.

There was a delay. First Harrison had to translate the question into more traditional English. Then in order to ensure Ivanov understood what he was dealing with, an interpreter from the entourage had to put it to him in Bulgarian. When it became clear that he did get the message he was visibly very angry. He rose. He thumped the table and he almost spat out the answer. "The Constitution of the Socialist Republic of Bulgaria," he roared, "does not give the right not to work!"

Ivanov had tried to portray Bulgaria as a workers' paradise. McTeague had ensured that Ivan had failed.

Robert's Contention

As the title of this book not only suggests but states, all the entries are supposed to be stories and I would contend that all of them are stories though I would concede that in the case of this contribution it is more of a 'cri de coeur.'

It is about a Requiem, a rather fine Requiem, as it came to pass.

One of our former University colleagues had died. Within the University he was not particularly well-known but those of us who had worked with him liked him very much. He had been a quiet man and had worked hard and well. He did his work conscientiously and his students never had occasion to complain or grumble about him. As already observed, he was a quiet man who devoted himself to his teaching, did little or no research, did not publish and was never promoted from the Lecturer grade.

And now he was dead. A group of us who, as it happened, all lived on the one side of town, met from time to time for lunch and gossip. Phones started ringing and it was quickly agreed that we should go to the Requiem.

The widow, who was a very fine, active and an up-and-about lady who had taught Drama before she retired, had arranged a memorable event. Firstly, the church itself was impressive. More: it was in leafy suburbia in a rather up-market part of the city. A small but very musical choir was in attendance and it was supplemented by both a harpist and a soloist, a soprano. The priest said the mass beautifully and effectively and in his quasi-panegyric spoke eloquently, thoughtfully and with demonstrably genuine compassion and sorrow.

Come the day five of us attended: two Catholics — one active, one not — and three Presbyterians — two of them stalwarts (one of them an elder) and another from the dominant group in Scotland, the Presbyterian Agnostics.

When it was all over, when the coffin had been carried up the centre aisle followed by the family and other principal mourners, when the congregation had made its exit, when the coffin had been placed in the hearse and we managed to have a quick word with the widow before the cortège had made its slow departure from the scene, then and only then did we make our way back to our car.

The car doors closed and locked, I took it on myself to make a two-statement pronouncement.

"That," I said, "was an exceptionally fine occasion, but that said, thank God that Robert Crampsey was not there!"

"What's Crampsey to do with it?" someone asked.

So I explained it. Robert Crampsey in addition to all his other wonderful attributes was an accomplished musician but he had continually complained that all too many British singers sang melodiously but in such a way that one could not make out the words. In this case, throughout the Mass I had been able to follow only the hymns I already knew.

Yet that was not the totality of Robert's case. On the contrary, he went on to argue that American artists were much more clear in their singing.

For my own part I wholly agree with my late friend. Only this very morning I heard a recording of Peggy Lee singing 'The Folks who live on the Hill'. It was magnificent – not least in the clarity of the expression. The same is true of Nat King Cole, of Crosby and Sinatra. It is even true of Dean Martin — even when he is giving voice to banal lines about the moon in the sky being akin to a big pizza pie.

Robert would have conceded that not every British singer is found wanting. An example of the satisfactory is Shirley Bassey singing 'Goldfinger'. But there are not enough of them!

Given that one agrees with the Crampsey case, the question then arises as to why things are as they are: why is it so, what caused it? Robert himself put it down to professionalism and training. For what it is worth, I would accept that in part, a substantial part, of it involves other factors such as better sound engineers across the pond. Or again, might one ask, somewhat uncharitably no doubt, whether American singers have a primary objective of catering to the audience whereas the Brits are more concerned with pleasing themselves. Here I think of the so-called bands which appear at wedding receptions and who are unashamedly pleasing themselves, to such an extent that when asked to turn down the decibel count, they refuse to comply. Worse: they are paid for this blatant self-indulgence.

Well, there is the Robert Crampsey contention. If it is still raining you can think it over or, better still, start an argument about it.

The Holyrood Garden Party

It is possible that this story is not true, but, then again, it is possible it is true. We just do not know! As to its provenance, all I can report is that I got it from the daughter of a friend who, in turn, said that she had obtained it from a University friend who was the daughter of the only man of import in the tale.

The gentleman was a restaurant owner who had three such businesses in Glasgow – one in the West End, one in Prince's Square and the third in the Merchant City. All three were popular and, consequently, all three were profitable. He had all three swinging along like a well-oiled Swiss clock while he in turn could take time out to play a lot of golf.

He was a member of the Hilton Park Club off the Carbeth Road and one day over a drink in the clubhouse, a friend observed that he should consider applying for the contract to provide the catering for one of the Garden Parties due to be held in the grounds of Holyrood Palace in Edinburgh. Our hero's response was to scoff at the idea, arguing that his businesses were small-fry activities whereas Holyrood was a massive undertaking. It was, he contended, a question of the economics of scale, of size: he was just not big enough even to contemplate such a venture.

His friend counter-argued that he was doing himself a disservice. In one sense no-one was big enough to handle it, yet, that said, there were three or four undertakings which till now had had it all to themselves. It was, he argued, a quasi-oligopolistic situation, adding that he knew for a fact that the Scottish Office was anxious to bring in some new undertakings just to keep the existing quartet on their toes; as it was, they were in danger of becoming complacent. Moreover, he went on to point out that no-one had an army of waitresses at his disposal. *Au contraire*: whoever was given the contract for the day simply advertised and drew on the army of ladies with black frocks and white aprons who miraculously appeared for Masonic, Rugby Club, Golf Club, F.P. and other such dinners throughout the Edinburgh dining season. Alternatively, instead of advertising, they could approach an agency. What the cartel lot could do, he could do. In short, his friend's text was: "Go thou and do likewise!"

The outcome was that the following spring he applied and to both his surprise and delight he was awarded the contract for one of the early Parties. He had found out that there were agencies which provided the ladies so he contacted them and they did just that.

When the lists of the ladies came in his friend offered to look at them. When he had done so, he reported that all was fine but for one possible difficulty which was that he had two ladies each called Reid and to make things even more difficult one was Jessie Reid and the other Janet Reid. Janet was douce in all regards. She was polite and spoke quite well. In short, she was reliable. Jessie on the other hand was a holy terror. "Don't, for goodness sake, put Jessie anywhere near the Royals' tent. Put Janet there."

Come the day the lines got crossed and it was a harassed and peeved Jessie who swept into the Royal tent, complete with her cream cake on a silver tray and all the while brandishing her silver tongs.

"Aw right, then," she half roared. "Who's fur ra gatta, eh?"

A lady-in-waiting turned to the Queen Mother. "Did you hear that woman, Ma'am? She is talking about Henley!"

That, then, is the story. If it is not true, it deserves to be true.

The Clarke Family

In 1934 when I was nine years old we moved from a two-apartment flat in the Gorbals to a three-apartment Corporation house in Govanhill. Once there I found to my delight that in our new location there was a bunch of lads who were more or less an age with myself. These were the boys who featured in the story of 'Uncle Willie's Favourite Tie' which appeared in the first book of these tales.

As the years passed and the war became more and more likely I found that I was seeing more of Harry Clarke. Notwithstanding our tender age, we found ourselves discussing the international situation and such movie-documentaries as 'The March of Time'. Harry had no interest in football and so some Saturday afternoons we would find ourselves trachling into town to a philatelists' shop in Renfrew Street where we could spend an hour and more before each of us could resolve how to spend our tuppence or threepence.

There were eight in the Clarke household. Mr Clarke was a pleasant man with a fine sense of humour. My mother told me that when he was younger he and a friend called Cambridge had appeared as a comedy act at concerts and the like. As she saw it, Clark and Cambridge were more amusing and more entertaining that Naughton and Gold who made it all the way to the Crazy Gang.

That, however, had been some years back. At the time I knew Mr Clarke he was a semi-skilled operative at the Singer's factory in Clydebank.

Mrs Clarke reminded me of the mother in the Broons family in *The Sunday Post*. Mrs Clarke was not as heavily-built as Mrs Broon but like her she was the dominant personality in the household.

They had four children – two boys and two girls. Both the girls worked in a biscuit factory in Kinning Park. Agnes, the older of the two, was a secretary to one of the managers while Isabel was a packer on the assembly line. James was the older of the two brothers and the oldest in the family. He suffered from curvature of the spine though people referred to him as a hunchback. He had gone to a 'Special' school for disabled children. He shone at school for, of course, there was nothing wrong with his brain.

Despite his being clever James left the school at 14 as they had no provision to take older children into higher learning. At the time of his leaving school the family lived in Norfolk Street very close to Gorbals Cross. He had written hundreds of job application – all to no avail.

One day when he was 15 and his mother was up to her elbows in soap suds while working in the common wash-house in their back-court, James appeared to report that he had been invited for interview by a firm in the city centre.

His mother expressed her delight but conveyed her concern about his disability. James placated her and explained that he had advised them of his handicap.

He went for interview and was offered the post of office-boy. When I came to know him he was in his middle to late thirties and was the Chief Accountant to the firm. James Clarke was one of the finest gentlemen I was to know. Like almost all with that disability he died in his middle fifties.

I said there were eight individuals in the Clarke household and I have accounted for six of them. The residual two were two brothers called McDonald who were nephews of Mrs Clarke. They had been orphaned when they were teenage boys. The second parent had died about the time the Clarkes had been allocated their four-apartment house in Govanhill and Mrs Clarke, observing that this was providential, immediately declared that she would take them with her to the new house. By the time I got to know them the older of the two was a printer working in the Corporation Printing Works to the north of Eglinton Toll while the younger of the two was a baker who started work at 6 a.m.

Mrs Clarke had succeeded in shoe-horning all eight of them into her house. The girls were in one of the two rooms designed as bedrooms. The other bedroom was used by all four of the young men, the Clarkes in one double bed and the McDonalds in another. This arrangement involved two wardrobes standing in the hall-way.

Harry Clarke left school at sixteen and started an apprenticeship at Singer's beside his father. Harry, however, was destined for the Drawing Office.

By the end of the war, and even before it, Mrs Clarke was in the fortunate position of having seven pay pokes coming into her each week. James, Agnes and the older McDonald were all making good to very good money while the other four – the father, Isabel, Harry and the younger McDonald were all contributing to the income flow.

It was all very changed days from Norfolk Street in the middle twenties when only Mr Clarke's modest pay had to sustain the six of them.

Affluence, even modest affluence, is attained by a variety of routes. In the case of the Clarkes there was no recourse to entrepreneurial activity but there was a preparedness to study and application. James by a steady use of evening classes and correspondence courses became a highly efficient and respected accountant.

Harry, as I remember it, did the same and took his A.I.Mech.E. and if we run ahead of ourselves, was to be a manager of a small to middle-sized engineering factory in East Kilbride. Agnes, as I remember, married her manager and went to live in Pollokshields.

Mr Clark went on working in his modest post at Singer's but threw a lot of his energy into the affairs of our Tenants' Association for which he organised an annual outing, at the time of the September Weekend, to Blackpool. At Social Evenings, he revived his old music hall attributes.

For their summer holidays the four 'boys' went to a camp at Douglas on the Isle of Man but James took command of the situation and had them aspiring to a modest hotel and then after two or three years to an impressive hotel on the sea front. As one of the McDonalds remarked, they had seen such comfort in films but had never even dreamed of actually experiencing it.

This situation of moderate affluence persisted throughout the immediate post-war years. Many items were in short supply but as and when they became available Mrs Clark was not slow in obtaining the latest gadget on the market. I can recall Harry not quite boasting but observing with not a little pride that in addition to normal roof-attached lighting they had nearly thirty electrical appliances in their house. This array of devices included two standard lamps, one in each public room; six table lamps, two of which were in the hallway; and four wall lamps in the bigger of the two public rooms. The list went on to include three radio sets, two gramophones, a radiogram and a television set and extended to a washing machine, a dishwasher, an electric kettle and two carpet sweepers and an electrical strip above the shaving mirror in the bathroom while the girls had a hair-drier in their bedroom. They had — they needed — two alarm clocks and they too were electrical.

Isabel was the first to leave the home. She married a bricklayer and went on to live in Crosshill. In the spring, summer and early autumn days her husband worked three nights a week on overtime rates and double time on Sundays. It did not seem to take long for their house to rival the Cloch Lighthouse in electrical power.

Harry who had been a devotee of youth hostels at his week-ends, moved up-market to a dearer and more comfortable arrangement at Dollarbeg in Eastern Clackmannanshire. There he met and in due course married Margaret Lauder who came from Kelvinside. It was not long till they bought a house in Jordanhill.

The McDonalds left, Agnes, as reported, marrying her manager.

When Mr Clark died, Mrs Clark and James were left on their own whereupon they moved to Mansewood – a top-level Corporation development somewhat further out from the City centre and a long way from Norfolk Street.

In writing these tales, I deliberated long and hard on whether or not to include the story of the Clarke family. As can be seen, I eventually decided to include it – and this for two reasons. The first was that I saw their story as a mini-case study of an economic and social transformation which happened to millions of British families from 1925 until 1965. The second reason was that knowing and being friendly with the Clarkes had a dramatic effect on my life and that tale within a tale I shall relate now.

The war started on Sunday 3rd September 1939. At first, things were rather uncertain. Some schools, for example, closed while others remained open, most cinemas closed and the black-out was introduced immediately. Some folk but not all went about carrying their gas-masks in their wee cardboard boxes. Together with other lads, Harry and I felt bereft, our world had been upset. Then, one night in November, Harry mentioned that his sister, Isabel, was a member of a Co-operative Youth Club which met twice a week in the Co-operative Halls in Coburg Street, back to back with the Co-operative Emporium in Eglinton Street. The Club met from 7.30 until 9.30. Tuesday evenings were devoted to games which consisted of a lot of table tennis, beetle drives and quiz nights. Meetings were held on Fridays and the agenda usually provided for both the business of the Club and time for a speaker who was usually a member of the Management Board of the Co-operative Society or of its Education Committee. The subscription was very low as the facilities were provided free by the Society's Education Committee. Harry suggested that we join the Club.

Here it should be explained that within a few weeks of our joining what Isabel called the Co-operative Comrades' Circle I had come to realise that this was not the single, one-off, isolated institution we had inferred from Isabel's reports to Harry, but was instead a branch of an organisation called the British Federation of Co-operative Youth, a national body working under the auspices of and surveillance of the Co-operative Union in Manchester. The age-group was ostensibly 16 to 25 but this it appeared was not rigorously applied.

Branches were substantially assisted by their local Co-operative Societies, but the body had its own structure which followed that of the wider Co-operative Movement and most left-wing organisations throughout the world: branches sent delegates to district committees which sent delegates to sectional bodies which sent representatives to a national committee.

Harry never took much interest in this structure. For years he was to be a good and active member but he never aspired to office-bearing even at branch level, whereas within a year of joining I found myself responsible for the social activities on Tuesday evenings. Then, when I was 16 and still at school, I came home one night to be told by my mother that a man called John King had called and left an attaché case for me as I had been appointed as Secretary of the Glasgow District Committee. More, before I left school and started work, I found myself appointed to the Editorial Board of our national magazine.

That situation continued through the two years or so of my employment in local government until my departure at the age of 18 to report to the R.A.F. with the view to take up training as a navigator in Bomber Command. While I was in the Air Force I contributed occasional articles to the magazine and on my release into Civvy Street in 1947 I returned to my branch of what had been restructured as the British Federation of Youth Co-operators – a small change in nomenclature but one which signified a considerable change in status within the Co-operative Movement. Immediately on demobilisation I was appointed to the Editorial Board of our magazine, which in turn involved four trips each year to London. Within months I found myself on the Scottish Sectional Committee and increasingly involved in Week-end Schools.

As the forties rolled over to the fifties our upper age level was increased to 28 but from the age of 25 onwards I found I was devoting more and more time to part-time study and serious courtship. I continued to write and help with the editing but my attendance at branch level diminished as did my involvement in the senior bodies.

In 1952 I was awarded a Diploma in Public Administration from the University of Glasgow and in 1956 a B.Sc. Econ. from that of London whereupon I started teaching Politics and Economics in the evenings. In 1961 I left the Civil Service and took a full-time teaching post at the Scottish College of Commerce. In 1962, I took my M.Sc.Econ. from the London School of Economics, started my association with the Salzburg Seminar in American Studies and was promoted to Senior Lecturer. In the winter of 62-63 I looked around for a subject to take for a possible Ph.D. and decided to research the history of the political wing of the Co-operative Movement. I submitted the dissertation in 1966. The Chairman at the ensuing viva was Sir Alexander Carr-Saunders, the former Director of the London School of Economics. Some eighteen months or so after I was awarded the Doctorate, Manchester University Press invited me to produce a popularised version of the thesis and this was duly published under the title 'Consumers in Politics'. Most of this was very pleasing and helped what we had come to regard as 'my career'. Success begot success.

There was, however, to be an even more dramatic turn.

One Friday evening in November of 1969 I arrived home to be told by my wife that a civil servant lady had phoned twice from London. She was a Miss Goose and wanted me to go to London to see a Minister. I was to phone her back.

My immediate reaction was one of scepticism. Earlier that day I had been teased by some colleagues about my knowledge of political matters and in particular the working of Government. Was the Miss Goose matter an extension of that teasing? Yet when I phoned, Miss Goose actually existed. She explained that their Minister (it was of Post and Telecommunications) wanted to see me on a matter which could be of advantage to me. Would I come to London? The day she suggested was one with a heavy teaching load so it was a non-runner. I suggested a quieter day when a friend could cover for me and we agreed on it. There was no mention of expenses: the inference was that I had to carry the cost of the fishing exercise.

On the day I met the Minister he wasted no time in coming to the heart of the matter. He had to make a recommendation to Downing Street of a Scot to join the Board of a rather important public body, a quango. At the recent Labour Party Conference he and some other Ministers had been rebuked for appointing too many venerable Tories to such posts. He had arranged for his staff to trawl over his appointments and recommendations: the charge was valid. His critics had been vindicated.

He had drawn up a list of four possibles of which I was one. He intended to see all four and then choose. The question at issue was whether I was prepared to be interviewed. I agreed and what followed was no perfunctory, put-you-by exercise. On the contrary, it lasted an hour and three quarters – as long as a football match plus half-time interval. He concluded by asking me whether I could give him three good reasons as to why I should be the winner. I said I could give him three reasons. It was for him to decide whether they were good reasons.

He never – or so I thought – mentioned the nature of the post though he alluded to the ITA which had left me wondering where the Initial Teaching Alphabet figured.

As I took my leave, he said that if it was to be me I would receive a very formal letter from Downing Street. If I was unsuccessful I would no doubt see from *The Glasgow Herald* and *The Scotsman* that someone else had been appointed.

In early December I was invited by the Prime Minister to become the Scottish member of the then Independent Television Authority which with the advent of commercial radio became the Independent Broadcasting Authority. The appointment was for five years but I was to be given two extensions and in total served for nine and a half years from January 1970 to August 1979. No-one was to serve longer.

My years on the Authority were to lead to other posts. These posts tended to lead to related appointments. Thus, in the wake of being on the IBA, I was appointed to the Broadcasting Complaints Commission and from it to the Press Council which pre-dated the Press Complaints Commission, while the work on the Press Council led to my being appointed as Ombudsman to two Scottish newspapers.

Most of these appointments were in the public sector. They included the Royal Commission on Gambling, the Scottish Legal Aid Board, the Data Protection Tribunal and the Scottish Consumer Council. All in all, my friends reckon that between 1970 and 2010 I served on over twenty quangos and other such public bodies.

It is this that brings us back to the Clarke family for, as I see it, all my involvement in these Government and quasi-Government appointments can be traced back to the appointments I secured and to the training I received in the British Federation of Co-operative Youth and later in the British Federation of Young Co-operators. All that would not have occurred as it did had it not been for Isabel and Harry Clarke persuading me to join the 'Club' which they recommended.

I was and I am highly indebted to the Clarkes.

Compassion and Venom

This is a short story, a very short story. Then again, it is as old as the hills. Yet despite that feature I find all sorts of folk who have never heard it and who, being discerning, enjoy it when they do.

I have encountered many versions but the setting of Lithgow's shipyard in Greenock seems to me to be the finest.

So we are told that the head of that company, Sir William Lithgow, was in a private hospital-cum-nursing home in Glasgow. He had undergone an emergency operation which had been very successful and he was now recuperating. Lady Lithgow was with him and she was giving him all the family news when a nurse came in, excused herself and reported that a working man called Alex Dunbar had called hoping to see Sir William.

"Not that dreadful Communist!" declared Lady Lithgow.

Sir William rebuked her gently. "Come, come, my dear," he said. "I have told you again and again, he's not a Communist. He's in the ILP."

Lady Lithgow was not to be chastised. "ILP, Communist, they are all the same," she declared.

"Thank God they are not," said her husband and turning to the nurse, thanked her and asked her to bring the gentleman in.

Dunbar came in, shoving his cloth cap into the pocket of his raincoat. "Good evening, Sir William, ma Lady," he opened. "It is good of you to see me, Sir. I wid explain that the Shop Stewards Convenors met this afternoon and I was instructed tae come up tae town tonight and convey oor collective best wishes fur a full and speedy recovery and oor hopes that it's no long till yer back in yer ain office."

"Most kind, Dunbar. Most kind," replied the Chairman.

"Not at all, Sir. Ah wiz only too glad tae dae it," he paused and went on. "An' anither thing, Sir William, ah thought ye should know that the motion was carried by nine votes tae seven wae twenty-three abstentions. Well, goodnight, Sir, ma Lady." Whereupon he took his leave.

I like that story very much. It rings true of the workforce-management relationship then. Better still: it brings out the compassion and the venom which permeated that delicate relationship.

Lightning Source UK Ltd.
Milton Keynes UK
UKOW05f0227260813

215971UK00001B/4/P